Penguin Books
The Return of Eva Perón

V. S. Naipaul was born in Trinidad in 1932. He came to England in 1950 to do a university course, and began to write, in London, in 1954. He has followed no other profession.

He is the author of *The Mystic Masseur* (1957; John Llewelyn Rhys Memorial Prize), *The Suffrage of Elvira* (1958), *Miguel Street* (1959; Somerset Maugham Award), *A House for Mr Biswas* (1961), *Mr Stone and the Knights Companion* (1963; Hawthornden Prize), *The Mimic Men* (1967; W. H. Smith Award, 1968). *A Flag on the Island* (1967), a collection of short stories, was followed by *The Loss of El Dorado* (1969) and three novels, *In a Free State* (1971; Booker Prize), *Guerrillas* (1975), *A Bend in the River* (1979) and his powerful new novel, *The Enigma of Arrival* (1987).

In 1960 he began to travel. *The Middle Passage* (1962) records his impressions of colonial society in the West Indies and South America. *An Area of Darkness* (1964) is a reflective and semi-autobiographical account of a year in India. *The Overcrowded Barracoon* (1972) is a selection of his longer essays, and *India: A Wounded Civilization* (1977) is a more analytical study – prompted by the 1975 emergency – of Indian attitudes. *The Return of Eva Perón with The Killings in Trinidad* (1980) contains studies of Argentina, the Congo and the Michael X killings, and *Among the Believers: An Islamic Journey* (1981) is the result of seven months' travel in 1979 and 1980 in Iran, Pakistan, Malaysia and Indonesia. *Finding the Centre* (1984) contains two personal narrative pieces about 'the process of writing. Both seek in different ways to admit the reader to that process.'

V. S. Naipaul

The Return of Eva Perón
with
The Killings in Trinidad

Penguin Books

Penguin Books Ltd, 27 Wrights Lane, London w8 5TZ (Publishing and Editorial)
and Harmondsworth, Middlesex, England (Distribution and Warehouse)
Viking Penguin Inc., 40 West 23rd Street, New York, New York 10010, USA
Penguin Books Australia Ltd, Ringwood, Victoria, Australia
Penguin Books Canada Ltd, 2801 John Street, Markham, Ontario, Canada L3R 1B4
Penguin Books (NZ) Ltd, 182–190 Wairau Road, Auckland 10, New Zealand

This collection first published in the USA by Alfred A. Knopf, Inc. 1980
First published in Great Britain by André Deutsch Ltd 1980
Published in Penguin Books 1981
Reprinted 1981, 1983, 1988

'The Mythical Founding of Buenos Aires' by Jorge Luis Borges, translated by
Alastair Reid, is taken from Borges: *Selected Poems, 1923–1967*, edited by
Norman Thomas di Giovanni (Allen Lane The Penguin Press, 1972)
Original Spanish texts copyright © Emecé Editores, S.A., Buenos Aires, 1954,
1958, 1960, 1964, 1966, 1967, 1969
English translations copyright © Emecé Editores, S.A., and Norman Thomas
di Giovanni, 1968, 1969, 1970, 1971, 1972

Printed and bound in Great Britain by
Cox & Wyman Ltd, Reading
Set in Linotype Baskerville

Author's Note

These pieces, except for additions made to 'Michael X' and to 'The Return of Eva Perón', were written between 1972 and 1975. They bridged a creative gap: from the end of 1970 to the end of 1973 no novel offered itself to me. That perhaps explains the intensity of some of the pieces, and their obsessional nature. The themes repeat, whether in Argentina, Trinidad or the Congo. I can claim no further unity for the pieces; though it should be said that, out of these journeys and writings, novels did in the end come to me. 'The Killings in Trinidad' was published, after many delays for legal reasons, in the London *Sunday Times*. Everything else was published in *The New York Review of Books*.

Contents

Michael X
and the Black Power Killings
in Trinidad

I

A corner file is a three-sided file, triangular in section, and it is used in Trinidad for sharpening cutlasses. On December 31st, 1971, in the country town of Arima, some eighteen miles from Port of Spain, Steve Yeates bought such a file, six inches long. Yeates, a thirty-three-year-old Negro, ex-R A F, was the bodyguard and companion of Michael de Freitas – also known as Michael X and Michael Abdul Malik. The file, bought from Cooblal's Hardware, cost a Trinidad dollar, 20p. It was charged to the account of 'Mr Abdhul Mallic, Arima', and Yeates signed the charge bill 'Muhammed Akbar'. This was Yeates's 'Muslim' name. In the Malik setup in Arima – the 'commune', the 'organization' – Yeates was Supreme Captain of the Fruit of Islam, as well as Lieutenant Colonel (and perhaps the only member) of Malik's Black Liberation Army.

Malik's 'commune' was a residential house in a suburban development called Christina Gardens. The house, which Malik had been renting for eleven months, ever since his return from England, was set in a one-and-a-half-acre plot. On this land, with its mature garden and mature fruit trees, Malik and his commune did 'agriculture'. Or so Malik reported to old associates in England and elsewhere.

Malik had spent fourteen years in England. He had gone there as Michael de Freitas, a Trinidad seaman, in 1957, when he was twenty-four. In Notting Hill, where he had settled, he had become a pimp, drug pusher and gambling-house operator; he had also worked as a strong-arm man for Rachman, the property racketeer, who specialized in slum properties, West Indian tenants and high rents. A religious–political 'conversion' had followed, and Michael de Freitas had given himself the name Michael X. He was an instant success with the press and the underground. He became Black Power 'leader', underground black 'poet', black 'writer'. In 1967, when he was at the peak of his newspaper fame, he was convicted under the Race Relations Act for an anti-white speech he had made at Reading, and sent to jail for a year. In 1969, with the help of a rich white patron, he had established his first commune, the Black House, an 'urban village' in Islington. This had failed. At the same time there was more trouble with the law. And in January 1971 Michael X – now with the Black Muslim name of Michael Abdul Malik – had fled to Trinidad.

The agricultural commune in Christina Gardens was not Malik's only 'project' in Trinidad. He was simultaneously working on a 'People's Store'. Letterheads had been printed, and copy prepared for a brochure: 'Empty shelves Shows the lack of Genorosity [*sic*] of the haves to the have nots ... The wall of honour bears the name of our heroes and those that give ... All praise is due to Allah the faults are ours.' The only thing that was missing was the store; but in a note on the scheme Malik had written: 'Public Relations are the key-words to success.' During his time in England Malik had learned a few things; he had, more particularly, acquired a way with words. In Trinidad he was not just a man who had run away from a criminal charge in England. He was a Black Muslim refugee from 'Babylon': he was in revolt against 'the industrialized complex'. Trinidad was far enough away; and so, in a country town, in the mature garden of a rented suburban house, Malik could say that he did agriculture, with his new commune.

On January 1st, 1972, the commune could be said to include two visitors, who were living in a rented house on the other side of the road. One was a Boston Negro in his late thirties who wore a gold earring and had given himself the Muslim name Hakim Jamal. The other was Gale Ann Benson, a twenty-seven-year-old middle-class English divorcee who had been living with Jamal for about a year.

Jamal was an American Black Power man. A few months before, when he was being taken around London by Gale Benson, he had described himself to the *Guardian* as 'excruciatingly handsome, tantalizingly brown, fiercely articulate'. That was his style. From Trinidad he wrote to a white associate in the United States: 'Money is a white people thing – the thing they protect. The heaviest thing they have to carry.' And Jamal was anxious to lighten the load: he was full of schemes for black uplift that needed white money; one such scheme had brought him down to the West Indies. He was in some ways like Malik. But Malik did black agriculture and black communes, and Jamal did black schools and black publishing; and the two men did not clash. Malik claimed that he was the best-known black man in the world; and Jamal appeared to agree. Jamal's own claim was that he himself was God. And Gale Benson outdid them both: she believed that Jamal was God.

This was Benson's distinction in the commune, her private cult of Jamal. Not her whiteness; there were other white people around, since for people like Malik there was no point in being black and angry unless occasionally there were white people to witness. Benson wore African-style clothes and had renamed herself Halé Kimga. This wasn't a Muslim or an African name, but an anagram of Gale and Hakim; and it suggests that in her madness there was an element of middle-class play.

Some weeks later Malik's wife told a reporter of the Trinidad *Evening News* that Benson was 'a very mysterious person'. She must have used the word ironically, because she went on: 'She was sort of a fake ... She will give a fake name and maintain her fake position.' A thirty-year-old black woman, a secondary-school teacher, said of Benson, 'She was pretty. Different. Simple. Money oozing out of the clothes.' White, secure, yet in her quiet middle-class way out-blacking them all: Benson could not have been indifferent to the effect she created. The absurd cult, the absurd name, the absurd clothes – everything that is remembered of Benson in Trinidad suggests the great uneducated vanity of the middle-class dropout.

But to be a fake among fakes: in the melodramatic atmosphere of the commune that was dangerous. She was alien, impenetrable. It was felt that she was an agent; there was talk of an especially secret branch of British Intelligence called M10. Her execution, on January 2nd, 1972, was sudden and swift. She was held by the neck and stabbed and stabbed. At that moment all the lunacy and play fell from her; she knew who she was then, and wanted to live. Perhaps the motive for the killing lay only in that: the surprise, a secure life ending in an extended moment of terror. She fought back; the cuts on her hands and arms would show how strongly she fought back. She had to be stabbed nine times. It was an especially deep wound at the base of the neck that stilled her; and then she was buried in her African-style clothes. She was not yet completely dead: dirt from her burial hole would work its way into her intestines.

In Trinidad at this time there was a young Indian fortune-teller, Lalsingh Harribance, whose uncanny and daring public prophecies were making news. *The Bomb*, a popular local weekly, carried an article about Harribance; and Malik, who had written for *The Bomb*, found out from the editor where Harribance lived.

Harribance lived in the south of the island, in the oil-field town of Fyzabad, a winding two-hour drive from Port of Spain. Malik went down with some members of his commune in two cars. That was Malik's travelling style in Trinidad – the 'retinue', the large American hired cars, the chauffeur. Rawle Maximin, a partner in the car-hire firm that Malik patronized, and a boyhood friend of Malik's, went with them. They got to Fyzabad late in the evening and were told that Harribance was at home but was seeing nobody. A seer's privilege. They decided to wait.

Rawle Maximin says they waited in the cars until morning. 'And just when I was thinking "You mean they not even sending out a little coffee or something?" Harribance sent out a woman with some coffee. And Michael got to see Harribance. And Harribance said to Michael, "You will not stay in Trinidad. You will go to Jamaica. And then you will be the ruler of the Negroes in the United States." But then he said to Michael as we were leaving, "I want to see you again." But Michael never saw Harribance again.'

Harribance, as it happened, very shortly afterwards joined the brain drain to the United States. An American woman married him; and the story in Trinidad is that Harribance is now at an American university helping with ESP research.

Patrick Chokolingo, the editor of *The Bomb*, has something to add to Maximin's story of the visit to Harribance. 'There was a pointed question to Harribance about hanging. I have this story from Harribance's cousin. Malik wanted to find out at all costs whether he would die by hanging. The answer was that he would *not* die by hanging.'

Many stories come up after an event. But it is possible that this prophecy – the promise of immunity and of further great success – explains something of what was to follow. *

In an inside page of the Trinidad *Guardian* of February 13th, 1972, there was a small, odd item: DIVERS FAIL TO FIND BODY. Steve Yeates   Muhammed Akbar, Supreme Captain of the Fruit of Islam, Lieutenant

* Writing from Sugarland, Texas, fifteen years later, in February 1987, Harribance said no question about hanging was put to him; and he made no prophecies about Malik. He was tired when Malik came; he asked him to come at another time for a reading. Malik, Harribance suggests, used the visit to make his own 'propaganda'. And, indeed, it would have been like Malik to fabricate a prophecy he needed and then to believe his fabrication.

Colonel of Malik's Black Liberation Army, the foreman of the Malik commune, Malik's bodyguard and familiar – had drowned.

He had drowned three days before at Sans Souci, which is known to all beach-going Trinidadians as one of the most dangerous bays on the rocky north-eastern coast. Around a small central shelf, which is reasonably calm, the current has gouged out deep holes in the sea floor; even a few feet from the shore, in waist-high water, it is not easy to keep one's footing; every breaking wave takes the bather out and to the west, to a litter of rocks, a long reef, and high, crashing waves. Bodies are seldom recovered from Sans Souci. Once they are swept beyond the reef, local fishermen say, they are eaten by the giant fish known as the grouper. There are safer bays before Sans Souci, at Balandra and at Mission; but it was at Sans Souci that the Malik party of eleven had stopped to bathe. Two of the girls had quickly got into trouble. Yeates had saved one, and had disappeared trying to save the other. A fishing boat had later gone out and rescued the second girl; but the body of Yeates hadn't been recovered.

What was odd about the item in the *Guardian* was that it was presented as a statement by Malik, two days after the event. Patrick Chokolingo, editor of *The Bomb*, didn't like the story. 'I thought it was funny – the way it was presented – because to me anybody associated with Malik was news, and this drowning deserved bigger treatment. I rang a few people and the police, and a police officer did mention to me that they suspected Malik had drowned Yeates – but this was very much an off-the-cuff statement. You can imagine my surprise when the following day Malik turned up in my office and he said he wanted me to do a story on Steve Yeates, a hero, who tried to save an Indian girl – Malik again, trying to squeeze some race out of it. Off the cuff I blurted out, "But, Michael, the police say you kill the man." And he said, "I don't care about what the police say." '

This was on Tuesday, February 15th. At 11.25 on Saturday night the Arima fire station heard that the Malik house in Arima was on fire. For a one-storey house with concrete floors and walls and a corrugated-iron roof, the fire was unexpectedly fierce. But the annexe at the back, separated from the main house by a concrete patio, wasn't touched; and everything that was stored in the annexe was intact: the African art objects that Malik had brought from England and on which he placed a value of £60,000 and the £400 piano, which was said to be a gift from John Lennon. A mysterious fire: no member of the commune was present, and Malik and all his family had flown out earlier in the day to Guyana.

That was a journey of some style. The travelling companion of the Malik family was a Guyanese Negro called McDavidson, fat and smooth-skinned, a sharp dresser, one of the ambitious nondescripts thrown up by the new politics of the region. McDavidson's wife was a minor minister in the Trinidad government, and his nephew was Junior Minister for Youth Affairs in the Guyana government. Malik had paid for McDavidson's ticket; McDavidson had spoken on the telephone to the office of the Guyana Prime Minister; and the Malik party, on their arrival in Guyana, was welcomed by the Junior Minister for Youth Affairs and driven away in two cars. Such a reception no doubt led to early press reports that Malik had gone to Guyana as a guest of the government to attend the second-anniversary celebrations of Guyana's 'Cooperative Republic', and that on Saturday evening he was among the dinner guests of Mr Burnham, the Guyana Prime Minister. These reports were quickly denied. What is true is that on Sunday Malik addressed some members of the Youth Socialist Movement, the 'youth wing' of Mr Burnham's political party.

In Arima the road that led to Malik's burned-out house had been barred off by light aluminium rails and patrolled by Negro and Indian policemen with automatic rifles (new to Trinidad, and called, because of the perforated barrel, 'see-through guns'). The fire commissioner suspected arson; the police were concerned about hidden arms.

At three o'clock on Tuesday afternoon the Trinidad police, searching the grounds of the house in Arima where Malik and his commune did agriculture, discovered a six-foot grave below a recently planted bed of lettuce, in the feathery shade of a flamboyant tree and beside a hedge of peach-coloured hibiscus. The grave was estimated to be seven to ten days old, and the body in blue jeans and a green jersey found in a sprawling position at the bottom was horribly decomposed, its sex not immediately apparent to the policemen or the professional gravediggers who had been called in, the face distorted and half melted away around bared teeth, one of which was capped in gold. The blue jeans were lowered: white underpants. Not a woman. A man, Negro or Negroid, five feet nine inches tall, whose head had been almost severed from his body.

But not Steve Yeates, whose death by drowning Malik had reported to the press just a week before. Steve's denture had no gold, his father said when he went with the police to the Port of Spain mortuary. Steve's hair was different; there was no need for his father to look for the large scar on the back, the relic of a fight Steve had had in England. Not Steve Yeates, an anonymous woman caller told *The Bomb* the next day: the body was that of another 'brother' in the 'organization'. 'The man died last week Monday night, and the whole thing was accidental. They did not go to kill him. Just beat him up ... He died foolishly as he won't abide by the rules of the organization.'

And that was not far wrong. The body was identified the day after as that of a twenty-five-year-old Port of Spain man, Joseph Skerritt, a man once charged with rape (like Steve Yeates himself) but otherwise quite undistinguished: the failure of his respectable lower-middle-class family, one of thousands of the city's half-educated young men, unemployed and superfluous, drifting through their twenties, idling in streets scrawled with empty slogans: BLACK IS IN, BASIC BLACK. Joe Skerritt had last been seen alive a fortnight before on February 7th. On that day Malik, with his retinue, had called at the Skerritt house in Port of Spain and taken Joe away to Arima.

Malik's house was the only one on the western side of the approach lane. To the north of the house, beyond a boundary line of young coconut trees and the high wire-mesh fence, there was a piece of wasteland, ending after two hundred feet or so in a narrow tree-hung ravine, its water slow and shallow and not fresh. On the southern bank of this ravine, two days after the discovery of the body of Joe Skerritt, a second grave was found. This grave was shallower, about four feet, and the smell was soon high. A blue dress with a flowered pattern, red panties, a twisted, decomposing body: Gale Benson.

She had been stabbed to death on January 2nd. And here, on the ravine bank, she had lain for more than seven weeks. And no one had missed her, not even the two English people who were visiting the commune at the time. But they no doubt had other things on their minds. Simmonds, the woman, well nourished, with big, widely spaced top teeth, told *The Bomb* that during her six weeks at the commune she had had 'total involvement' with Steve Yeates: Muhammed Akbar, Supreme Captain of the Fruit of Islam, who on December 31st (before the public holiday on January 1st) had gone to Cooblal's Hardware and bought a six-inch corner file.

And Jamal – Benson's master – what had Hakim Jamal done? Simmonds remembered that one morning in January, after they had all dined together the previous evening, Jamal had said that he and Benson had had a quarrel and Benson had gone away. And that was that. Eighteen days later Jamal left the Malik commune to return to the United States. He didn't leave alone. He left with the 'co-worker' he had summoned down from the United States in mid-December, a man who had remained in the background, and of whom little was remembered: an American Negro known in the commune by the African-sounding name of Kidhogo or Kidogo.

In Trinidad now there were many rumours of fresh finds at the commune; one rumour was that a tinful of mixed penises had been found. But the ground had given up its dead. Six men were charged with the two murders. Five were Trinidadian; one was American. This wasn't Jamal, but his co-worker Kidogo. Kidogo was one of the five charged with the murder of Benson. Kidogo was in hiding in the United States. Jamal gave interviews, and now he was as sober and anxious to survive as everybody else. He spoke of 'the atmosphere of violence' at the commune; he said he was lucky to be alive; he said he would like to see Malik and ask him a few questions about Benson.

So, in sobriety and self-absolution, the Malik commune ended. The ground had been dug up, the house burned out. All that remained were the two Malik dogs, bewildered, never barking or whining, restless, scampering about the grounds and the road, excited by the sound of every stopping car. But no car brought the people they were looking for.

In Guyana, Malik was on the run. McDavidson, who had travelled with the Malik family from Trinidad and had, as uncle of the Junior Minister for Youth Affairs, arranged their reception in Guyana, McDavidson shaved off Malik's Black Power beard and trimmed his hair. Someone else went to get new clothes and a new pair of shoes; and Malik, in his new outfit, had booked in under another name – perhaps 'Mr T. Thompson' – at another hotel. Michael de Freitas, Michael X, Michael Abdul Malik, and now Mr Thompson, Mr Lindsay, Joseph, George. So many names, so many personalties, so many ways of presenting himself to people: that was his great talent, but now, at the end, he was close to breakdown.

He stayed for three days in the hotel, the curtains always closed in his room. He told the Indian chambermaid that he had malaria and couldn't stand the sunlight. He ordered nothing from the bar or the kitchens. The chambermaid went out to buy him sandwiches and soft drinks, paper and two ballpoint pens. He had important messages for various people. He was only a 'middleman', he had told McDavidson; the really important man, the man with the 'massive plan', was coming down soon from the United States to meet him in Guyana. The chambermaid, taking in a flask of iced water, for which he had asked, saw him 'writing letters'. But he wasn't happy using the ballpoint pen; he would have preferred a tape recorder. In the darkened hotel room he became obsessed with the need for a tape recorder, and once he nearly telephoned his wife to bring him one. 'I wanted,' he said later, 'to record on tape all the things that had happened to me. I wanted to get it on record.' Words were important to him; he had lived by words. Words could give shape to an event, and words were never more important than they were now.

In England there were people who had told him that he was a writer, even a poet; and often, in a marijuana haze ('I am high I love it'), he had tried to be a writer, writing out the marijuana mood in a page or two and coming to a halt. In these writings fact and fiction sometimes flowed together. With words he remade his past; words also gave him a pattern for the future. And, bizarrely, he had once written of an adventure that was like the one he was having in Guyana.

The narrator, who may be Malik himself, is on the run. With only twenty pounds in his pocket, he is taken in by someone called Frank and told he can stay for six months. That night the narrator sleeps and has no nightmares. Then the door opens. 'My Friend My saviour Frank, with a [indistinct] breakfast and a Newspaper, all smiles. You in the paper today he says, and I panic again, they found me. I think [indistinct] more. Let me see! I say there was I not too bad a picture and a short story. One of Trinidad's more famous sons returns home to finish writing his novel. In an Exclusive Interview at — and it goes on and on, I smile relieved the Journalists here have an Imagination like anywhere else —' Here the fragment ends.

But in Guyana the nightmare did not break. The reports in the Guyana newspapers, which he was reading in the hotel, were getting worse. And two days after the discovery of the body of Gale Benson he left the hotel, took a taxi south to the bauxite town of Mackenzie (now called Linden, after the first name of Mr Burnham, the Guyana Prime Minister), and then, in his new long-sleeved blue shirt and red-checked short trousers, with an airline bag containing some of his hotel writings (some he had left behind in the hotel room), some Guyana ten-dollar notes, biscuits, milk, sardines and other tinned food, and with a piece of cutlass, he headed for the interior, along the south-west trail.

Two hundred miles away, beyond the forest and the brown savanna land with the giant anthills, lay the Brazilian border. It seemed that he was making for this, but later he said: 'I knew of a person in the interior who was a good and wise person to counsel with. I thought I would find this person ... I have always been to counsel with people who can see things. You have a man here in Trinidad called Harribance. I go to him. I like these people. I thought I would go to this person and counsel with him and find out what is happening because it was not something I could reason out.'

He was on the trail for three days. He was now barefooted: the new shoes that had been bought for him in the capital didn't fit or had become too painful. About four or five in the afternoon of the third day he saw two Land-Rovers. Government Land-Rovers: a survey team: a camp. He waited for two or three hours. About half-past seven he went to the men in the camp. He said, 'Good night, gentlemen,' and introduced himself as a journalist. They gave him a cup of coffee. He said – too vaguely – that he wanted to go 'down the trail'; and after about half an hour he and a man called Caesar and another man left the camp in a Land-Rover.

Malik asked Caesar about the road to Brazil, and about his religion. Caesar, a handsome man, big and very black, said he belonged to a local Africanist group which was something like a Black Power group. Malik – the X again – said that police all over the world were looking for him. But then he must have had an intimation of betrayal. And his mind worked fast. He said there were two messages he wanted Caesar to take back to Georgetown, the capital. One was for Mrs Malik: Caesar was to tell her that he, Malik, was safe. The other message was for Caesar's Black Power Leader: Caesar was to tell him that there was a police informer in the group.

After five or six miles Malik, who had become restless, was set down at a place called Bishop's Camp. Bishop was a small elderly Negro, a solitary in his bush 'farm'; and his 'camp' was two thatched shelters, one with no walls. He gave Malik some stew-and-rice and 'sweet broom' herb tea. Thousands of police were after him, Malik said; and Bishop said (the real-life adventure, now in an unexpected forest setting, echoing that scrap of Malik's man-on-the-run fiction) that Malik could stay in the camp for the rest of the year.

Malik was tired, and during this last night of freedom his talk was disordered. He asked repeatedly about Brazil, and his safety in the camp; he said he had no faith in

Caesar. He remembered the Trinidad commune, and that fantasy of 'agriculture' became fact. He said he would teach Bishop 'how to grow greens'. He said he wanted a job: he could 'plant'. Bishop should plant mustard and celery in boxes and after three weeks plant them out eighteen inches apart. He asked Bishop if the river was far. Bishop said it wasn't far; but Malik said he would show Bishop how to get water from the river without walking to the river. He remembered England, and especially Rachman, the slum landlord for whom he had worked in the early days in London; and Bishop must have been puzzled. To Bishop it seemed that Malik was saying that he had owned a big boarding-house in London, with a big garden, that he had kept a big dog and a revolver, and that when tenants couldn't pay he had put them out, but that he had always been nice to Guyanese.

Bishop made up a low 'cot' for Malik in the open shelter. Malik, lying down, seemed to groan. He said his feet were cold; Bishop gave him a sack for his feet. Malik presently fell asleep. But Bishop didn't sleep: he was frightened of Malik's 'piece of cutlass'. All night he watched Malik.

At about half-past five, when it was still dark, the camp dogs barked, and Bishop saw the police; Caesar was with them. They surrounded the shelter and waited. It quickly became light, and 'the form of a fair-skin man lying on the lower or western cot' became distinct to the police superintendent. At five to six they began to close in. Bishop, still watchful, pointed to Malik's airline bag and cutlass. At six, daybreak, the superintendent tapped Malik and awakened him.

When he saw the police he was, as he said later, relieved. His feet were hurting; he doubted whether he could walk. He was taken to Georgetown; the next day he was declared an undesirable immigrant and flown back to Trinidad.

*

The discovery of the body of Gale Benson had been the sensation; but the first inquiry was about the killing of Joseph Skerritt, who had been buried below the lettuce patch, and it was for the murder of Skerritt that Malik and three of his commune were tried four months later. When the grave was discovered, an anonymous woman caller had told *The Bomb* that the body, then not yet identified, was that of a 'brother' who had failed to 'abide by the rules of the organization'. And Skerritt's killing was indeed in the nature of an execution.

Malik was uneducated, but people in England had told him that he was a writer; and he did his best to write. There were also people who had told him – ponce, con man – that he was a leader (though only of Negroes). So he had read books on leadership; and once, borrowing a good deal from what he had read, he had even written a paper on the subject. 'I have no need to play an ego game,' he wrote, explaining his position, 'for I am the Best Known Black man in this entire [white western world *deleted*] country.' Leaders were workers, doers, finders of tools, 'be it money, hammers or saws': the 'masses' came of their own accord to such leaders. But it was not always pleasant to be a leader. 'Leaders are feared even by those closest to him ... and others will envy him ... here one needs an Iron Hand for one may be tempted to placate the doubter with a gift, and the only real gift one can give is silence.' Borrowed words, almost certainly; but Malik was made by words. And Joe Skerritt was a doubter.

The previous year, when Skerritt had been charged with rape, he had gone to Malik for help, and Malik had talked the girl out of making trouble for Skerritt. But then Skerritt had become uneasy with Malik; he began to hide from him; and to Mrs Skerritt it even seemed that her son was being ungrateful. At last, on February 7th, Malik came with some of his commune to the Skerritt house in Port of Spain; and they took away Joe with them to Arima 'for a few days'.

Skerritt loafed about the garden that day, doing the odd jobs. In the evening he and three of the commune got into a hired car and went for a drive. When they were on the Arima–Port of Spain highway, Abbott, the driver, said they were going to raid a police station for arms. Skerritt said he wanted none of that; and Abbott immediately drove back to Christina Gardens. Malik said, 'Joe, boy, you say you ready for work, and now that I've sent you to work, you refuse to go?' He looked at Skerritt and shook his head, and said to the man escorting Skerritt to his sleeping quarters that he should give Joe a Bible or something to read.

A sudden decision, it would seem; but – from the evidence given at the trial – what followed was well planned. In the morning Steve Yeates drove Mrs Malik and her children to Port of Spain. That wasn't unusual. Malik announced that the commune was going to dig a 'soakaway' that day. That wasn't unexpected. The ground flooded easily; a soakaway helped drainage, and Malik had taken advice from a qualified man about soakaways. A pit had to be dug down to where the soil changed; and then it was to be filled in with a bottom layer of stones and a top layer of earth.

So all morning – Malik from time to time interrupting his 'writing' in the 'study' to superintend – some men dug and two others brought jeeploads of stones to the house. Joe Skerritt, in his 'old clothes', jeans and a green jersey, helped with a wheelbarrow, taking the stones from where the jeep dropped them to the far north-western corner of the garden. At about one o'clock the pit was deep enough. Malik told the two men in the jeep to go and 'cool off' at a farm they all knew and then to bring a load of manure.

When they left, there remained in the garden Malik, three men, and Joe Skerritt. One of the three men walked away from the hole. Malik, with his revolver in a shoulder holster, and with a cutlass in his hand, went down into

the pit and said to Abbott, 'I am ready. Bring him.'
Abbott locked his arm around Skerritt's neck and jumped
with him into the pit. Malik, using his left hand to hold
Skerritt by his long Afro hair, chopped him on the neck
and then, still with his left hand, threw him aside. The
gesture, of 'contempt', appalled Abbott. Skerritt cried
out, 'Oh, God! Oh, God!' and began stumbling about
the pit. Malik, now out of the pit, lifted a large soakaway
stone with both hands and brought it down on Skerritt's
head, and Skerritt, close to death, cried out like a child,
'I go tell! I go tell!' Malik hurled three or four more
stones at Skerritt, and then Skerritt was quiet. Then
the four men – the fourth man called back to help –
began to fill in the pit, the stones below, the earth on
top.

When the two men returned with the jeepload of
manure from the farm, they saw that the stones had
disappeared, the soakaway was half filled in; they helped
finish the filling in. And when presently the Malik
family returned from Port of Spain, the commune was the
commune again. As for Skerritt, 'the strange young man'
who had turned up the day before, he had just gone away
again. The foolish boy had gone to Canada or the United
States, but he was going to find things hard 'outside':
that was what Mrs Skerritt was told. And that, at the
trial, was Malik's story: that Joe Skerritt had just disappeared.

Abbott, who had jumped with Skerritt into the pit,
was sentenced to twenty years. Malik was condemned
to hang. Some people stood by him. One of them was
Rawle Maximin, a boyhood friend, the garage owner
whose cars Malik had often hired. Maximin visited Malik
at the Royal Gaol in Port of Spain. One day, many
months later, when he was waiting for the verdict on his
appeal, Malik said to Maximin, 'You were with me that
day when I went to see Harribance. Can you remember

what Harribance said?' 'He hadn't forgotten,' Maximin says. 'He just wanted to hear me say it. So I said to him, "Harribance told you that you would leave Trinidad and go to Jamaica, and then you will be the ruler of the Negroes in the United States." And he said, "Good, good." And began to pace up and down that little cell.'

To be the ruler of Negroes: so that, at the end, for Malik and his well-wishers abroad (mainly white, and they continued to send him money), Negroes existed only that Malik might be their leader. Malik saw himself as a man who had always risen: a semi-educated Port of Spain idler, one of thousands; then a seaman; then a Notting Hill pimp and gangster; then the X of London; then, at thirty-seven, 'the Best Known Black man in this entire white western world'. It was as a London success that he had come back to Trinidad in January 1971. 'I'm not here to make my way,' he told the Trinidad *Express*. 'I've made that already.' But he believed he could 'help'. 'I'm not interested in elections and stuff like that. The only politics I ever understood is the politics of revolution – the politics of change, the politics of a completely new system.'

Revolution, change, system: London words, London abstractions, capable of supporting any meaning Malik – already reassembling his gang, his 'commune' – chose to give them. There were people in London who were expecting Malik, their very own and complete Negro, to establish a new government in Trinidad. There had been a meeting; someone had made a record. The new government was going to underwrite the first International University of the Alternative, 'the seat of the counter-culture of the Alternative'. Words, and more words: 'I cannot go into details,' Malik had said. 'But I can say this. The new university will be an experimental laboratory of a new and sane life-style.' But – the eternal warning of the X, the eternal thrill and flattery – the white

28

people who came to Malik's Trinidad (an airbus service
was promised to all international capitals) had to remember that there was 'a just hatred of the white man' in
the heart of every black; and they had somehow to get
over the fact that they 'belonged to the race of the
oppressors'.

The leader, the unique spokesman of Negroes dangerous with a just hatred; but the crowds at his trial were
good-humoured, even gay. No one jeered; he was a
martyr to no cause. Only Simmonds, the white woman
who had had 'total involvement' with Steve Yeates during
her six weeks at the commune, only Simmonds, flying
down from England, gave the photographers a clenched-
fist salute; but she had a return air ticket. To the Trinidad crowds Malik had become a 'character', a Carnival
figure, a dummy Judas to be beaten through the streets
on Good Friday. Which was all that he had been in
London, even in the great days of his newspaper fame as
the X: the militant who was only an entertainer, the
leader who had no followers, the Black Power man who
was neither powerful nor black. He wasn't even black;
he was 'a fair-skin man', half white. That, in the Trinidad
phrase, was the sweetest part of the joke.

2

It was in London that Malik became a Negro. And
perhaps only someone who knew that he wasn't really a
Negro – someone who knew that when the time came he
could go off and play another game – could have worked
so hard at the role, and so guyed it. He was shallow and
unoriginal; but he sensed that in England, provincial,
rich and very secure, race was, to Right and Left, a topic
of entertainment. And he became an entertainer.

He was the X, the militant, the man threatening the

fire next time; he was also the dope peddler, the pimp. He was everybody's Negro, and not too Negroid. He had two ideas of his own. One was that the West Indian High Commissions in London paid too little attention to their nationals. The other, more bizarre, was that the uniform of the Trinidad police should be changed; and this was less an idea than an obsession. Everything else was borrowed, every attitude, every statement: from the adoption of the X and the conversion to Islam, down to the criticism of white liberals ('destroying the black man') and the black bourgeois ('they don't know the man from the ghetto'). He was the total 1960s Negro, in a London setting; and his very absence of originality, his plasticity, his ability to give people the kind of Negro they wanted, made him acceptable to journalists.

'Michael X once told me,' Richard Neville writes in *Playpower*, 'that hippies were the only whites his people could talk to.' And Malik was always willing to be instructed in his Negro role. Late in 1965, when he was working on his autobiography (subsequently ghosted by an Englishman, and published in 1968 under the title of *From Michael de Freitas to Michael X*), he sent the manuscript to an English adviser, and received a long memorandum in reply. '... At this juncture you may look at the negro's relationship with the whiteman throughout the world. Use South Africa, Rhodesia, England, Portugal and America to speak of the heartlessness of white society. Use slavery, use the recent massacre of the Jews at Auschwitz and Belsen ... *Chapter 15* You ought to close powerfully, frighteningly perhaps, on "This I Believe". Your own true statement of one displaced black man in this particular context of history ...'

So cliché led to cliché. And, inevitably, the racial clichés that Malik was led to, via the 'counterculture', were sometimes pre-revolutionary. Once, aiming no doubt at the underground press, he wrote a kind of parable about an Anglo-Saxon called Harold, a Jew called Jack, and a Negro, who was himself. 'All we have in common is two hands, two feet a head. I must admit mines are infinitly nicer to look at for their bodies are covered with a sickly pale whitish skin and even they can recognize it for what it is. Harold expressed a desire early in our talk to go somewhere in the sun and transform. I see his point for when he was saying this I followed his eyes caressing my beautiful golden brown skin my inheritance from my African [*insertion*: and Portuguese] forefathers.'

It is a 'difficult task for three people of as diverse Racial Charisterics as ourselves to truly communicate'. But they are good friends, and agree to talk of their 'most secret desires'. Harold the Anglo-Saxon wants to search for truth. 'Jacks not as simple as that': Jack the Jew wants to 'make things for people, the people he's closest to are naturally his own people, Jews he will make whatever they need, money, Clothes, Factories'. And Malik, the Negro, sees 'the great divides that exist between us of diffrent Races for my own search is one of happiness to create Joys for myself and others to hear Laughter, to give ... But what a strange dilima this throws us into when I give to him the seeker after truth my humble present and he in his search looks into my little gesture for a deeper motivation or Jack when he makes a garment, and I say how lovely, could I have one and he tells me x Pounds.'

Malik's ghosted autobiography was a publishing failure; one of his white patrons bought up most of the copies. The tone of the book is determinedly gay; there are lots of sex and parties – the ghost, easily turning oppressed blacks into abandoned spooks, seems in places to have excited himself with thoughts of a Michael X musical. But it is not an easy book to read.

It is not the story of a life or the development of a personality. The narrator, from his London eminence as the X, the reformed Negro ponce who is now the Negro leader, assumes that the events of his life are well

31

known; and he is concerned only to present himself in all his Negro roles. Events accumulate confusedly around him; he is without a personality; he is only a haphazard succession of roles. On page 116 – at the time of his meeting with an unidentified young property millionaire, who is interested in art – the narrator appears, without warning, as a painter ('my abstracts and surrealist portraits'); and he supports this role for exactly seventeen lines. Equally sudden, equally successful, and almost as brief, are his manifestations as Negro poet, writer, and even as a teacher of 'basic English' at something called the London Free School.

The only other considerable figure in the autobiography is Malik's mother; and she is as puzzling as Malik. She appears first of all as a ferocious old-fashioned black woman, concerned about appearances and forever preaching the beauty of whiteness. She doesn't like her son to play with black children or to get his hands dirty; she is snobbish; when she goes to the Port of Spain market she refuses to speak French patois to the *marchandes* and insists that her son speak English; she sends her son to an 'exclusive' school. This is overstated, but it has a certain logic. But then, just twenty pages later, the mother is suddenly a drunkard, hysterical, quarrelsome, wearing appalling Negro-woman's clothes. One day her son finds her sleeping in the fowl coop, which she says she has converted. Suddenly she is a 'hustler'; suddenly, coming to London, she is transformed into a successful and jolly brothelkeeper.

The childhood of the leader, the rebel who learned to love black, no longer makes sense; the emphasis is wrong. Certain facts about his mother are too important to the narrator for him to leave out. But the facts have been scattered about the picaresque narrative: a pain greater than the one stated is being concealed. When the facts are put together, the childhood of the leader can be interpreted in quite another way.

Malik's father was a Portuguese shopkeeper who later

left Trinidad to do business on the island of St Kitts. His mother was an uneducated black woman from Barbados. In Trinidad, and especially in the tight lower-middle-class Negro community of Belmont in Port of Spain, she was a stranger, with different manners and a different accent. If she didn't speak the local French patois it was because she didn't know it. She was a stranger with a 'red bastard', and she was never allowed to forget it by the black taxi driver with whom she lived. (He used to tell her that all she had got from the Portuguese man was a big cunt and a red bastard. This is not in the autobiography; it was part of Malik's statement at his trial.)

The mother was disgraced by the son; the son, growing up in Port of Spain, going to St Mary's College (a major school, but not so 'exclusive': the fees were just over three pounds a term), his home life known to all, was disgraced by the mother. She was uneducated, drunken, vicious; they tormented one another. He fled from her whenever he could, going off into the hills with his friends. Once he got all her clothes together and burned them. But she pursued him everywhere with her public scenes, even after he had been expelled from the college, even after he had grown up. He could escape only by leaving Trinidad, by becoming a seaman; at one time he thought of going to live in Guyana. In the end he went to England; but she followed him even there, getting off the boat train at Waterloo in a red bathrobe.

In 1965, when his London fame was beginning, and when in his own eyes he had made good, Malik began a letter to his mother.

London, April 1st, 1965

Dear Mamma,

My hand is shaking and my head hurts, I want to tell you a few things, for I am not afraid anymore, I am a negro, you told me I was different, its not true, I tried to be. I was ashamed not of being a negro but

33

of you. I would like first to tell you what made me write this last year. I was at home and Steve rang me, he asked me if I knew what happened to you, Well you were arrested. At sixty odd years of age for running a Brothel, this I could of tried to understand, I would of blamed anybody for this, the white man, my father, myself, but when you gave your name as de Freitas because as you said you wanted to protect your own name, that was the end. Its x months since that day and I have only just recovered enough to say something about it. I don't hate you, that is impossible to do, I would like to think that was a thoughtless action but I said all the other horrible things you did were thoughtless too, you have humiliated me once too often, you usually give a lot of thought to things before you do them remember in Trinidad when you were still living with your husband and you threw boiling water on him in bed, you thought that one out didn't you, you must off ...

She had got into bed with the man, and when he was asleep she had got out; she had heated the water beforehand. The incident doesn't appear in the autobiography Everything else does; but in the padded-out, picaresque narrative, the passion and the pain vanish, simplified, and vitally altered, to give a smoother account of the boyhood of the leader.

This letter is the truest thing Malik ever wrote, and the most moving. It explains so much: the change of name from de Freitas to X, the assumption of so many personalities, the anxiety to please. A real torment was buried in the clowning of the racial entertainer. Black Power gave order and logic to the life; it provided Malik with a complete system. He couldn't write a book; but it was better for him to say, as he does in the preliminary note to his autobiography, that the book was ghosted because black English is different from white English.

*

A London journalist who had some hand in the making of Malik says, 'Michael took the press for a ride, and vice versa. And out of it grew a monster.' The monster already existed; but there is something in the judgement. Malik was made in England. England gave him friends, a knowledge of elegance, a newspaper fame which was like regard, and money. England always gave him money; no one, for so many good black causes, needed money so badly. It occurred to him, for instance, late in 1966, when his wife was in arrears with her mortgage payments and receiving solicitor's letters, that West Indians needed adequate representation in the courts. He interested people in this cause. The London *Oz* of February 1967 announced the West Indian legal need, and in heavy letters at the top of the page prescribed the remedy: ' "Defence" needs money. Send to Michael Abdul Malik, Leith Mansions, Grantully Road, W9.'

England made many things easy for Malik. But England in the end undid him. Malik exaggerated the importance of his newspaper fame. He exaggerated the importance of the fringe groups which seemed to have made room for him. He was an entertainer, a play-actor; but he wasn't the only one. He failed to understand that section of the middle class that knows only that it is secure, has no views, only reflexes and scattered irritations, and sometimes indulges in play: the people who keep up with 'revolution' as with the theatre, the revolutionaries who visit centres of revolution, but with return air tickets, the people for whom Malik's kind of Black Power was an exotic but safe brothel. Malik thought he shared the security of his supporters. One day, half doodling ('No Money'), half jotting down memoranda ('Letter from Lawyer'), he wrote: 'My inheritance is London – all of it.'

His fame didn't last long. It began in 1965, and came to an end in 1967, when he went to gaol for an offence under the 1965 Race Relations Act. It was in July 1965 that Colin McGlashan, in a major article in the *Observer*, told of the existence in England of a militant black organization, the Racial Adjustment Action Society (RAAS), with a membership of more than 45,000, that had been created 'in near-secrecy' by Michael de Freitas. 'Some immigrants,' McGlashan reported, 'already talk of Michael X.' It was a good story: '... revolutionary fervour ... near-national organization ... formidable professionalism ... underground technique ... system of cells ... financed from donations and Mr de Freitas's own money ... organizers, in the best revolutionary tradition, accept a pittance ... a shy, gentle and highly intelligent man ... the authentic voice of black bitterness ... Says a friend: "It is a crime against humanity that people like Michael happen ..."'

It was a good story, and if it was a string of newspaper clichés it was only because what was being presented to McGlashan, as a good story, was a string of newspaper clichés. From his autobiography, published three years later, it seems that at the time of the McGlashan article Malik was perhaps more concerned with a beautiful white widow, whom he calls Carmen. Carmen was thirty, 'with a lovely, supple body', and rich. Once she opened her handbag and gave Malik 'a bundle of £10 notes'; another time she wrote him a cheque for £500. He took all that she gave – 'I have no doubt that the ponce element produced in the black man by the ghetto was with me that night' – but it was all for the cause, the Racial Adjustment Action Society. Still, he suffered: 'My speeches became more and more bitter.' And there was Nancy, another white woman, who was his steady. Carmen had to go. 'With the departure of Carmen, RAAS had no more income.' And in four pages, which also cover the story of Carmen, the membership of RAAS drops from 65,000 'on paper' to 2,000 'hard core'.

Malik loved his publicity. He cut out and filed every

reference to himself in the British press, however slight, however critical (the *Daily Telegraph* must have been his favourite paper). He filed two copies of McGlashan's article; and when he brought out his R A A S brochure – which was really a brochure about Michael X, complete with press notices (no other name was mentioned) – he used two separate quotes from McGlashan, together with quotes from the *Daily Mirror*, the *Daily Telegraph*, the *Sunday Times, Peace News*, and the *New York Times* ('Students, intellectuals, moderates and radicals are all being wooed. Some have already been won over').

R A A S was of course a joke. The initials spell out an obscenity which is Jamaican (and not Trinidadian) and is nothing more than a corruption of 'arse'. A crude joke, and in the autobiography it is grotesquely extended. 'In the first place R A A S is a West Indian word for a menstrual blood cloth. It has some symbolic significance in view of the way the black man has been drained of his life blood for so long. In the second place there is the similar African word *ras* (from the Arabic *ra's* – head) meaning Ruler or Leader.' A 'satirical' joke; but it could only have been made by a man who felt that he could, when the time came, withdraw from his Negro role.

Malik's Negro was, in fact, a grotesque: not American, not West Indian, but an American caricatured by a red man from Trinidad for a British audience. West Indians are not black Americans. American blacks are an excluded minority. West Indians come from countries with black majorities and black administrations; they have a kind of political tradition. Boscoe Holder, a black Trinidad dancer who was in London at the time, says, 'When I heard about this X guy I thought, "There goes one of our con men." And I wished him well, because he was in England and because they told me he was Trinidadian.' It was the West Indian attitude: the jester was re-

cognized and accepted as a jester, but was otherwise
kept at a distance. Occasionally Malik's publicity excited a student or a writer or a politician. In 1965,
after the McGlashan article, the leader of the Trinidad
opposition – mainly an Indian party – thought of
asking Malik down to Trinidad to help with the elections.

But Malik never held these people. And in London he
didn't really need them. A West Indian Malik had
recently met – and who was eventually to act as his political deputy – was a young Trinidadian called Stanley
Abbott, like Malik a college boy who had dropped out,
and like Malik a red man with Spanish or Portuguese
antecedents (Abbott sometimes called himself De Piva).
Abbott had come to England at the age of nineteen in
1956, and was very quickly adrift in London, a lost
soul adding and adding to a police record: wilful
damage in 1956, breaking and entering in 1958, Bor-
stal and supervision between 1958 and 1962, assault in
1964.

And already the West Indian closest to Malik was
Steve Yeates, black but in other respects a man like
Malik himself, a dropout from Malik's own Belmont
district in Port of Spain: Steve Yeates, soon to be given
the Black Muslim name of Muhammed Akbar, who had
been expelled from St Mary's College, Malik's old school,
for getting a fourteen-year-old girl from a Carmelite
reform school pregnant; Steve Yeates who, later, at the
age of sixteen, while he was a student at another college,
had been charged with nine others for the gang-rape of
a girl in the Girl Guides hut in Belmont; who, acquitted
but disgraced, had been sent by his family to England,
where he had joined the R A F, but had then got into
trouble of some sort and gone absent without leave; who
had been badly wounded in the back during a fight and
carried the scar.

The absence of responsible West Indian support ought

38

to have told against Malik. But he turned it to his advantage; American Black Power had provided him with a complete system. If educated West Indians wanted nothing to do with Malik, it was only because the black bourgeoisie and intelligentsia, 'a tiny minority within a minority', had cut themselves off from 'the man in the ghetto'. In Malik's system, the Negro who had not dropped out, who was educated, had a skill or a profession, was not quite a Negro; there was no need for anyone to come to terms with him. The real Negro was more elemental. He lived in a place called 'the ghetto', which was awful but had its enviable gaieties; and in the ghetto the Negro lived close to crime. He was a ponce or a drug peddler; he begged and stole; he was that attractive Negro; and now this Negro was very angry. The real Negro, as it turned out, was someone like Malik; and only Malik could be his spokesman.

Malik's revolutionary Negro was in many ways the familiar crapshooting spook. But it was a construct for a provincial market, and Malik's instinct about the kind of Negro the British newspapers wanted or would tolerate was sound. In the *Guardian* for August 9th, 1971, Jill Tweedie made the limits of British tolerance plain.

Tweedie did two Negroes for her page that day. One was Annie P. Barden, a 'school counsellor' at an all-black elementary school in Washington, D.C. Tweedie gave her a rough time. Annie Barden wanted to talk about her work; Tweedie wanted to hear about race and drugs and black militancy. They showed films about drugs, Annie Barden said; they 'talked through' things like slavery and the position of blacks in the South; she hadn't sensed any militancy in her pupils (some of whom were four, and none older than thirteen). But what about Malcolm X and Martin Luther King? How had Annie Barden herself become aware of race prejudice? Had things really changed? How many Americans regarded the black as a human being? The majority? Half? Were there *any* jobs for her pupils? The professions mightn't be closed to blacks, but wasn't it more difficult for them? At the suggestion, now amounting to insistence, that she was a Negro and her teaching job therefore a waste of time, Annie Barden offered her interviewer tea. 'She is evidently embarrassed,' Tweedie noted, 'by the whole question.'

For her other Negro, a man, Tweedie had a lot more time, and space. He was an American Black Muslim and he was in England to 'promote' his autobiography. It wasn't clear what he did for a living. He had started a Malcolm X Montessori school in California, but he didn't teach at the school because he hated white people – 'No S S man could invest the word "Jew" with any more contempt,' Tweedie noted – and he didn't want his hate to rub off on two-year-olds. 'If you're going to kill, it must mean something. You should kill people because they are evil, not because they are white ... They call me a nigger but I've invented my own kind of nigger. My nigger is me, excruciatingly handsome, tantalizingly brown, fiercely articulate.' Tweedie was taken: 'This black man is a handsome man, a brigand with a gold ring in his ear ... tall and spare and stoned on agro, sometimes overt, sometimes spread over with honeyed words about as sweet to receive as a punch in the kidneys. With a woman the agro comes masked, translated into sexual terms ...'

'Personally,' Tweedie concluded, 'I find Miss Barden's passivity far more depressing than Hakim Jamal's anger, and far less hopeful for the future.' Hakim Jamal – that was the name of the brigand with the gold earring. The autobiography he had come to England to sell was a conformist and very late addition to the Negro autobiographies of the 1960s: poverty and self-hate, drugs, Islam, reform, celebrities, sex, hate. His claim that he was God had won him an 'odd spot' appearance on the *World at One* radio programme. But he apparently hadn't told Tweedie that he was God. And if he didn't teach at his Malcolm X school it was because it had lasted one year, with one teacher, had closed down fifteen months before, and existed now only in the brochures he carried around with him. As for Annie Barden, she no doubt went back to her elementary school in Washington, and counselled a thousand pupils.

Malik's instinct, in the late 1960s (the Tweedie article appeared in 1971), about the kind of Negro that was wanted was sound. But the role was a consuming one. The black rebel, even if he wanted to, couldn't do a job; he couldn't appear to be declining into 'passivity'; anything like repose could extinguish his reputation. No one expected him to act out his threats, but the poor black was required ceaselessly to perform.

In July 1967 Malik – filling in for the more internationally known Stokely Carmichael – went to Reading and spoke to a mixed group of about seventy. 'If ever you see a white man laying a hand on your black woman, kill him immediately.' It was quite harmless, just the usual cabaret. But Malik was charged under the Race Relations Act. At his trial he told the recorder to sit down and 'cool it'; he had the Koran wiped with warm water before he swore on it; and he was allowed to perform Islamic 'ablutions' before giving evidence. He was sent to gaol for a year. All the newspaper reports of his trial were cut out and filed for him. But the carnival was abruptly over.

In April 1965, at the start of his great fame, he had written to his mother: 'I am not afraid anymore.' All the torment of his early life had been submerged in his role as the racial entertainer. Now his bluff had been called. His Black Power was no power in England, his newspaper fame offered no security. His ghosted autobiography, *From Michael de Freitas to Michael X*, came out while he was in gaol and was poorly reviewed. The publicity

41

declined. His release eight months later, though noted by television, was scarcely an event. A carnival element persisted: outside the prison gates there was a welcoming Negro who, refining on the X business, had given himself the name of Freddie Y. But Malik had changed.

He planned a second volume of autobiography. The title he first thought of was *My Years with R A A S* – the old Malik, the old joke. But as his mind darkened he changed that to *Requiem for an Illusion*. What was the illusion? England? His idea of his place in England? His career as the X?

From a long (at least fifty pages) and primitive novel he later began to write about himself, it is clear that he had begun to secrete a resentment, soon settling into hatred, not of white people or English people, but of the English middle class he had got to know: the people with money or connections who patronized him in both senses of the word, who were secure, who could fix anything, who held Negroes in contempt but were fascinated by him. In his novel, which is a childlike grafting of fantasy to fact (he is himself, with his own name), he has this middle-class English fascination turn to awe, perhaps even to love, and then, unexpectedly, to physical alarm. The setting isn't London, but Guyana. Malik has made himself a hero in that country, a great orator, and there are people in the streets who shout for him to be king.

It is hard, with Malik, to speak of a plan; he was a man who moved from event to event. But it seems that when he came out of gaol his thoughts turned to real power. In 1968 he joined the Black Eagles, a Negro fantasy outfit intended as a Notting Hill version of the Black Panthers. Malcolm X, Michael X; Black Panthers, Black Eagles. The 'prime minister' of the Eagles was a former Trinidad steelbandsman who had given himself the name of Darcus Awonsu. Malik became his 'minister without portfolio' and got a trip to Canada in a chartered aeroplane, to attend a Black Writers Conference in Montreal. Minister, writer; and now he found he had a reputation with Chicago and Toronto blacks as the only man in England to have gone to gaol under the Race Relations Act. 'Travelling first found out I was Hero': this is from the notes for *Requiem for an Illusion*, and it also says something about his attitude to his earlier career as the ponce X. 'Hero Image greater overseas.' He had somehow made it: he began to think that he was 'the Best Known Black man in [the] ... world'.

There was further proof the next year. Nigel Samuel, the son of a property millionaire, offered money for a 'Black House' project in Islington. A number of shops and offices, acquired on a twenty-one-year lease, were to be converted into a black 'urban village'. It was a coup: the demonstration of the creative, 'Panther'-like side of the black revolutionary. But Malik had no talents. To believe in the Black House was to believe in magic; it was to share Malik's half-belief (the con man's semi-lunacy, which makes him so convincing) that words and publicity made real the thing publicized. Within a year the Black House was failing; and like Hakim Jamal's Malcolm X school, like R A A S, like the Black Eagles, like the ventures of so many Negroes who act not out of a sense of vocation but trap themselves into performing, as Negroes, for an alien audience, the Black House existed only in its brochures and letterheads.

'Emergence of American Prototype like Panthers – with home base wanting carbon copy whereas the nation encourage self.' This is from the notes for *Requiem*. It reads like an attempt to rationalize the failure of the Black House, to suggest that it was part of his plan. But Malik was trying many things that year; he had begun to look beyond England. He had travelled with Nigel Samuel to Timbuktu in a chartered aeroplane, and later they had gone to Guinea to see Stokely Carmichael. He had sent a not very literate emissary to the O A U in

Addis Ababa. And he and Steve Yeates and, fleetingly, Nigel Samuel had gone to Trinidad. Kingship called for a black country. Everything was now pointing to an eventual return to Trinidad.

Trinidad in 1969 was moving towards a revolution. The black government of Eric Williams had been in power since 1956; and something like the racial enthusiasm that had taken him to power now seemed about to sweep him away. Political life in the newly independent island was stagnant; intellectuals felt shut out by the new men of the new politics; and American Black Power, drifting down to Trinidad, was giving a new twist to popular discontents. Black Power in the United States was the protest of an ill-equipped minority. In Trinidad, with its fifty-five per cent black population, with the Asian and other minorities already excluded from government, Black Power became something else, added something very old to rational protest: a mystical sense of race, a millenarian expectation of imminent redemption.

A revolution without a programme, without a head: it was something Malik might have exploited. But he didn't make much of a political start. He 'marched' with some striking bus drivers, but he puzzled them when he spoke, not of their cause, but of one of his obsessions: the need to change the uniform of the Trinidad police.

There was also talk of a 'commune'. Randolph Rawlins, a left-wing Trinidad journalist and academic, a man wearied by the simplicities and cynicism of West Indian racial politics, went one Sunday to the beach house, the site of the planned commune, where Malik was staying. Malik played tapes of Stokely Carmichael's speeches. Steve Yeates was there, and a 'retinue' of young men. 'They were totally subservient,' Rawlins says, 'and would react immediately. Malik's daughter was sick. He said to one of the men: "Go and get a doctor." The chap said he didn't know where to find a doctor. Malik said: "*Go* and get the doctor." I got tired of sitting down and seeing this man look ominous and talking rubbish. I adjourned to the sea.'

Already, though, a 'retinue' in Trinidad; and when Malik and his family followed Nigel Samuel back to England, Steve Yeates stayed behind. After thirteen years in England, Yeates had come home for good. Letters from Malik – busy in London with the Black House, busy with Nigel Samuel in Africa – were infrequent that year, 1969. In October Malik sent regards to 'all of the Brothers' and promised a second visit by Samuel; in November he announced his imminent return, with a party of thirteen. Nothing happened, but Steve Yeates waited. One day his father, who ran a little bar in Belmont, asked him about his relationship with Malik, and he said: 'It's a long story, pappy.' A long story: Steve Yeates, black, fine-featured, with 'soft hair, soft curly hair you felt you wanted to touch', but now with the English scar on his back, and now with the Black Muslim name of Muhammed Akbar, Supreme Captain of the Fruit of Islam, Lieutenant Colonel in Malik's Black Liberation Army.

A black woman who had known him in the old days, when 'he was the love of all the little girls in Belmont', fell in with him again.

He said he would never go back to England. He never spoke much about his life in London or his time in the air force. He used to tell me that I wouldn't talk to him if I had known him in London. Steve had lots of friends, but when he came back from London he was a loner. He didn't like parties or where there were too many people. He walked. Every night. As long as he was in Port of Spain he walked around the Savannah. Sometimes he would stop and have a coconut-water. Sometimes, if I was with him, he would sit on a bench and chat. He wasn't working, but he always had money. He had told me he was an aircraft mechanic. I asked him why he didn't get a job with one of the airlines. He said he didn't want to be tied down. He never told me what his views were, but he read a lot. Castro, Che Guevara. At one time he seemed to be in on this black scene. But then he would tell you he was living with this white woman and had two children with this woman, and you couldn't understand where he was going to and coming from. He was kinda bored. At times he would be waiting for a call, and this coded call would come. He was definitely waiting on Michael. We broke up in 1970. Just like that. The last time I saw him was Carnival night.

With the Carnival that year in Trinidad there came the Black Power revolution that had been maturing. There were daily anti-government marches in Port of Spain; revolutionary pamphlets appeared everywhere, even in schools; sections of the regiment declared for the marchers. Even the Asian countryside began to be infected. A spontaneous, anarchic outburst: a humane society divided in its wish for order and its various visions of redemption. But the police held firm; there was no need for Venezuelans or Americans to land. The outburst died down.

Steve Yeates took no part in these events. And Malik was later to say unkind things about the revolution. 'I cannot understand people who are hell-bent on all kinds of political nonsense,' the Trinidad *Express* reported him as saying. 'They want power or the trappings of power, but that entails hard work.'

This was now his line, and perhaps also his delusion: that his time in England had been a time of work, that he had become the best-known black man in the world through work, and that there were lots of bogus Negroes about who wanted to reap without sowing. It was his way of rebutting those who had begun to criticize his handling of Black House money. And it was also his way of saying that though he had missed the revolution in Trinidad, he was its true leader. Negroes existed now only that Malik might lead them: life hadn't caught up with art, but play had ceased to be play: through jest and fraud, disappointment and self-deception, Malik had reached the position that every racist power-seeker occupies. And it can be no coincidence that in March 1970, immediately after the Trinidad revolution, he started on his largest fund-raising exercise, to make the big killing before his return to Trinidad.

He announced a Black House Building Programme Appeal. The Bishop of London was asked for his 'learned advice' about the 'spiritual needs' of 'the many thousands who will be participating in the Black House'. A more direct appeal was made to Charles Clore: '... a fantastic world famous reality ... unique project ... let us show the world that Britain is not prepared to be a drop-out in the great race of culture and progress ...'

At the same time Malik consulted Patricia East of Patrick East Associates (International Public Relations), who did the P R for Sammy Davis, Jr., in England; and East offered to handle the account 'personally'. The Black House, she said, should be registered at once as a charity. She thought they should aim at setting up a string of Black Houses throughout the country. And she outlined a campaign which would, among other things, 'promote the name of Michael X as a household word for the good of the community at large'. There was a further point. For her services East required £3,500 (exclusive of expenses) for the first year, payable quarterly and in advance. This wasn't perhaps what was expected; and East, as she now says, 'lost touch' with Malik.

He went to work on his own. A standard begging

letter on the theme of 'Peace and Love' was devised: '... The difference in culture should not prevent men from living in peace. The men of culture are true apostles of equality.' A more businesslike letter went to Canada Life Assurance; they said no. Charter Consolidated said no, twice. A reminder was sent to Charles Clore, who hadn't replied; and now Clore's secretary said no.

It must have occurred to Malik at this stage that there was something wrong with his 'image'. Canon Collins was invited by 'Brother Francis (Director, Planning and Development)' to pay another visit to the Black House, 'this time at least for lunch'. And Malik drafted letters – 'Dear Brother' – to the presidents of the university unions of Cambridge, Oxford, Reading, Swansea, Cardiff, Edinburgh and Glasgow, and asked to be invited to speak on Black Power or the Alternative Society. He claimed to have spoken at most of those universities 'about three years ago'; he referred jocularly to his gaol sentence; he used words like 'confab' and 'relate with'; in his letter to Edinburgh he said he was mentioning the names of Alex Trocchi, Ronnie Laing and Jim Haynes 'as friends because it is possible that the only one you know me by could be Michael X'.

At the same time, as a Muslim, 'a worker and producer', a builder of a mosque, a converter of the infidel and a trainer of the young ('we are able to train in excess of 500 directly and an unresearched multiple indirectly'), he was making an assault on the treasury of the Emir of Kuwait. He wrote to the Kuwait Student Union and asked to be invited to Kuwait: 'As an articulator for our people I am invited to speak by all of our major universities in England.' He sent an autographed copy of his ghosted autobiography to the Kuwait embassy and, no doubt for reasons of drama, asked for it to be packaged in the presence of an embassy official and sent by diplomatic carrier to the Emir, together with a letter. He wrote two letters to the Kuwait ambassador. One asked for an 'audience even if it is only for five minutes', and drew attention to the second letter, which had been put in an envelope marked 'X'. X marked the spot: 'As you know, the biggest property owners in this country are Jews. Our landlords are Jews. We must get them off our backs ... We ask you to deal with this our request of direct financial aid as an urgent and top priority matter. In terms of money the figure of £100,000 (one hundred thousand pounds) is a very realistic and immediate need ... Yours in Islam, Michael Abdul Malik.'

It was as another kind of Muslim, Harlem and very devout, that he wrote to his Black Muslim contacts in the United States. He reported success ('an urban village ... a beautiful place to live in'); he confessed his fears about the Jews. But he reversed the Kuwaiti approach. The hard request came first; the flannel followed. 'We need most desperately, a large injection of capital ... Sometimes I feel very much abandoned and alone when I preach the word of the Messanger [sic]. Sometimes, when our need is very great and there seems no way to turn a Brother who has never spoken to the Holy Apostle [sic] would say to me "Why dont you bare your heart to him, surely he will help." But somewhere in my head and maybe this is because I had the honour to sit with him and look in his eyes, I feel that it is my duty to go out and search for our needs in the wilderness of Babylon.'

Later, in a statement at his trial, Malik summed up this period. 'I returned to the United Kingdom and started winding up my business, liquidizing certain of the assets that my family had acquired for the many years we spent in Europe.'

He encouraged some of the people around him to believe that he was successfully liquidizing: money or the show of money would win him those 'recruits' he was looking for. But he went too far. Like a man touched by the fantasies of his own begging letters, he began to speak of fantastic sums; and he trapped himself. He said he had got £250,000 from Nigel Samuel for the Black House; and there were people who believed him. (In the *Sunday Times* of March 12th, 1972, the 'Insight' reporters gave an outside figure of £15,000.) But the Black House had little to show for £250,000; in February 1970 a cheque for £237 to the London Electricity Board had bounced; and it began to occur to some people, during this fund-raising year, that Malik might be preparing to get away to Trinidad with the equivalent of a million Trinidad dollars.

'... Within found out that threats become Real – like being shot at – Problems with Black and Whites on organization.' The notes for *Requiem for an Illusion* are cryptic. But, as in the autobiography, Malik distorts one story by fragmenting it into many scattered stories; and the notes themselves later provide the key. 'Relation with outside – myth of immense wealth – How did this come about.' Malik was beginning to feel that in London he was close to danger. And even later, in Trinidad, he was never to lose the fear – perhaps some threat had been made – that his children might be kidnapped.

And there was trouble with the law again. Earlier in the year Malik and seven of his followers had been charged with demanding money with menaces from a London businessman – 'a local Jewish businessman', Malik had written to a Black Muslim in the United States. It was a complicated story about an employment agency, a black American, a job, a ring pledged in lieu of a fee. The sum involved was small, five pounds. But the businessman had been led about the Black House in a dog collar, and the case had attracted attention. Malik, for some reason, had written to the New China News Agency asking them to take an interest in the case; but what had appeared 'farcical' became less so when in

November Malik and five of his men were committed for trial at the Old Bailey.

Flight to Trinidad was now urgent. But Black Power had provided Malik with a complete system; even at this stage he made it fit. He gave interviews; he went on television; and he spoke now like a Black Panther. He was giving up Black Power, he said; henceforth he was going to devote himself to constructive work. He handed over the management of the Black House to Stanley Abbott, a fellow Trinidadian to whom – in the absence of Steve Yeates in Trinidad – Malik had grown especially close during the past year: Abbott of the pale complexion and the dreamy, bruised eyes, five feet six, neat and powerful, with a straight back and immensely muscular arms. Abbott was now thirty-three, fifteen years away from home, with a life already in ruins, with fresh convictions during the two previous years for possessing marijuana, for theft and for assault. Abbott believed that Nigel Samuel had given £250,000; Abbott believed that Malik was rich, and Abbott was loyal.

All was now set for Malik's flight to Trinidad. Steve Yeates was there, waiting, a bodyguard. But then Malik, remembering the Black Power revolution that had failed in Trinidad, remembering the Stokely Carmichael tapes he had played and the strikers he had marched with, became anxious about how he might be received. One day, playing records to 'mood' him, 'for this city is full of – and viciousness and I want to feel clean and talk the truth', he began to write to Eric Williams, the Trinidad Prime Minister. The letter quickly became hysterical, marijuana-hazy, and spread through a long postscript to seventeen pages.

He wrote, as he had so often written, to explain himself. The bewilderment of his early life had turned, with success, to awe at himself; he could put so many patterns on his disordered experience. And now, once again, he spoke of the poverty of his boyhood; of his name of de

Freitas ('there was so much dirt with him'); of his Notting Hill success ('I ran the most successful string of Gaming house and Whore houses that any Black person ever did in England'); of his great fame ('I know my name is a household word': the Patricia East P R proposals 'to promote the name of Michael X as a household word' had clearly made an impression on him).

As he wrote, his awe at himself grew. He saw himself 'living in danger on the real front line', and from this military metaphor he developed a fantasy about his life in England:

> Up here we are walking a tightrope, at the moment its like a suicide mission, you cannot come to our aid Militarily but here we can aid you they cannot Bomb London, Birmingham Liverpool etc. to get us, it must be man to man, we are ready. There are 52,000 English troops in Germany the Reserves are low, the Irish conflict contained enough explosive Power to draw 9,000 out of Germany, and they were ill equipped, I don't know how much longer we can hold out, A few weeks ago they were talking of Gas Ovens in the English Parliament but our morale is high.

So many personalities during this last year in England, so many voices: the real man had long ago been lost. Yet, promoting himself as a Negro, he everywhere 'passed'.

The Black House, after three weeks under Stanley Abbott, ended in chaos, in a general looting. And with that, Malik's London career was over. Abbott saw Malik the night before Malik left. From a pile of five-pound notes Malik gave Abbott two hundred pounds. 'Liquidized' assets: a glimpse of real money. When later, from Trinidad, Malik sent Abbott a letter with the one word 'Come', Abbott would take the next plane out.

3

After fourteen years his London career had ended in flight, and it might have been thought that he was finished. But Malik flourished in Trinidad as a free man for one year.

Trinidad in 1971 was his perfect setting. Trinidad, with its oil economy, was rich, with a standard of living equalled in South America only by Venezuela and Argentina. Every consumer comfort was at hand, and Malik was soon pleasantly settled in the country town of Arima, in a newish house with a large garden. But Trinidad was far away. In London, Chicago and Toronto, fund-raising centres, Trinidad could pass as an impoverished island where a black leader, fleeing persecution, and also reacting against 'the industrialized complex', might settle down, in a 'commune', to constructive work with despairing blacks, who needed only this leadership, and little gifts of money, to get started in black agriculture, black fruit-growing. And, later, even a little black fishing: a trawler (obtainable through 'contractural relationships with ... Schichting-Werft shipyard, Travemuende') would cost £18,000, but 'initial feasibility studies indicate that the profits ... would exceed £30,000 a month'. Remote Trinidad held this kind of possibility for its enthralled blacks; all that was needed was the leadership.

And in Trinidad Malik presented himself as a London success. Shortly after he came he sought out Raoul Pantin of the Trinidad *Express*. 'He wanted me to do this interview. I was to prepare both the questions and the answers, and I was to make it sound good. He was hiring a skill. His comment when I resisted this was: "How do you think I became famous if I couldn't find people in England to do this for me?" ' Some people were also shown a letter purporting to come from an English lawyer, in which the writer said that Malik couldn't expect a fair trial in England. Malik was also a friend of the famous. The names weren't always known in Trinidad and could be mangled – Feliks Topolski becoming Saponski or Topalowski, painter of the Queen, Alex Trocchi becoming Trotsky – and there were people who thought that Malik might only be a name-dropper. But the well-publicized visit in April 1971 of John Lennon as Malik's house-guest stilled all doubts.

He was successful; he had money; he had style. Rawle Maximin was a partner in the car-hire firm Malik now patronized. Maximin is a big, handsome man, half Indian, half Venezuelan, with no racial anxieties and no interest in the subject. But his business success, perhaps greater than he expected, now makes Maximin wish he were better educated; and he remembers Malik as someone who never made him feel less than a man.

Michael impress me a lot when he come back. He always move in a big way. If they are selling orange juice in that bar there for a dollar a glass and they are selling the same orange juice in that other bar for two dollars, he want the two-dollars one. If you go to the supermarket with him he fulling up two trolleys, one with meat only. You only hearing these slabs of meat dropping in the basket like iron – you know how they freeze and hard. He don't want all he buy and you know some of it will go rotten. But he want people around to see. Another thing. He never argue your price. And as friendly as we were he would never say, 'Lend me that car'. He would say, 'How much for that car?' He had his own car but he would hire mine, for the show. He want this crowd around him. 'I am the leader'. I liked him very much. He never made me feel less than a man. And he always give. I still have a pair of black socks of his.

Style, and money, were also noted by a black woman, a teacher, who went up to the Malik house in Arima at a time when there was some talk that she might teach the Malik children, who, because of the fear of kidnapping, couldn't be sent to school.

If you ran out of cigarettes you weren't offered a pack. You were offered a carton. Soft drinks by the case. Michael talked about the prices he had paid for this and that, and talked about the dogs he was bringing down from London. I was impressed by the décor of the house. You could see money oozing out of everything. You walked into a room, you saw taste. The house was very clean, everything well chosen and put away.

The local Belmont boy, with the common black mother who wore washerwoman's clothes, had made good. And with his success there had come a change in his manner. Patrick Chokolingo, editor of *The Bomb*, had met Malik in London in 1969, at the beginning of his fame. 'He told me that the white man was a devil. I said to him, "But you are living in a white man's country and you are part white." He said, "That may be so. But my heart is black. They made it black." He did capture me; he did excite me.' Shortly after Malik's return to Trinidad in January 1971, Chokolingo went to see him at the Chagacabana Hotel.

He was occupying one of the cabanas, and with him was Steve Yeates. I found he was trying to impress me – which I didn't think that time in London. He was selling me Michael, and his entire demeanour had changed. In the Marble Arch flat in London he had looked a little bit wild, a little bit fanatical, excitable, moving about in fits and jerks. In Trinidad he sat cross-legged in a reclining chair and his voice had changed. It had become very soft and persuasive. This was the first thing that struck me – that I was talking to a completely different person.

The new light voice, the relaxed manner: other people noticed the change as well. Malik was made by words, his and other people's. He needed a model always, and a clue to his new manner may be provided by the ghosted autobiography of 1968. Malik doesn't say much about Rachman, the London property racketeer for whom he worked as a strong-arm man. But what he says is oddly admiring. Rachman, in his book, is cool and stylish, almost a Hollywood character, 'a good-looking man with a strong face'. He is introduced, Hollywood-fashion, sitting at a desk, surrounded by his Alsatians, and with two bodyguards, one just sitting, one reading a newspaper. 'He was very well dressed and groomed and spoke in a quiet voice which I never heard him raise. In short, he exuded quiet charm.' Rachman, in Notting Hill, was in his 'manor'. It might be that Malik, in Trinidad, fancied that he was in his.

Chokolingo asked Malik to write for *The Bomb*, and found that he was 'pushing at an open door'. Malik began a series on brothels. 'He would not be satisfied, he said, until he had wiped brothels off the face of Trinidad. He did not see how Chinese men could come here and destroy the little girls of Trinidad. He was particularly aiming his barbs at the Korean Chinese who were running brothels in Port of Spain. Two were prosecuted. One hanged himself in his cell.' But then the police came to Chokolingo and told him it was a shakedown: Malik had raised 10,000 Trinidad dollars, £2,000, from two brothel operators. Rich Trinidad, demoralized by years of racial politics, and tense after the Black Power upheaval of 1970, offered this kind of possibility. Later, when he had settled in, Malik thought of a £50,000 'foundation', to be named after his wife; and he prepared a list of local people who might be asked to contribute.

And he didn't neglect the 'agricultural' side. Chokolingo says:

Sometime in '71 he went up to Toronto and Chicago, and one day I got a call from Michael in Toronto. He said, 'Do you remember that worm that was destroying the cabbages of the dirt-farmers on the Highway?' Worm? Cabbages? And then I realized that he had an audience at the other end, and I said, 'Oh yes. Yes.' And he said, 'Well, I've got the people at the University of' – I can't remember – 'who are prepared to investigate this, and I would like you to put some of those worms in a bottle and mail it to me at this address.' The next time it was from Chicago. That time I was a little wiser. 'That project we were discussing about those farmers and their arid lands on the east coast – I've got some people who are prepared to move the silt from Orinoco basin and deposit it in this area. So you can pass the message on to the farmers.' Shortly after he came back he started to splurge. He bought a Humber Super Snipe and a jeep.

And in Trinidad the 'commune' grew. No agricultural commune grew so fast; on no kibbutz did fruit trees mature so swiftly. Within months, from his suburban garden, Malik was reporting to a correspondent in the United States on the expanding commune's need for 'more moving equipment – another tractor, a bulldozer', claiming at the same time 'a |sic| impressive surplus of coconuts, limes, oranges, grapefruit, mangoes, milk, Anthorium [sic] lilies, cow and horse manure'.

He had an option to buy the Arima house at the end of the year – the £1,000 he had paid was in effect a year's rent – but people believed the house was his. One day he told a visitor – the black woman teacher – that he had also bought the large French-style house at the back and was going to have it redecorated. Ringo Starr was the next Beatle coming down, and that was where he would stay. He looked over a £4,000 piece of land in Guanapo, in the hills to the north; he didn't buy, but he later 'incorporated' it into his commune as 'extra land acquisition

... able to absorb from the U.S. initially sixty young men and women on a construction redevelopment programme.'

In Carenage, a seaside slum settlement west of Port of Spain, he rented a £35-a-month house from Oswald Chesterfield McDavidson, the black Guyanese entrepreneur involved with things like beauty competitions who was the husband of a Trinidad government minister. This house was 'The People's Store'. Its 'trustees' were Steve Yeates and Stanley Abbott and it handled the 'produce' of the commune. Letterheads had been printed and copy prepared for a brochure. According to this, the profits of the store were to be handed over each month to a different black cause.

In Arima itself there was a racing stud farm, owned by a Portuguese who was another Belmont boyhood friend, and with whom Malik now struck up a relationship. That was also 'incorporated' into the commune: it was the source of the milk and the manure that formed part of the commune's 'impressive surplus'.

Everything in Malik's commune existed; nothing belonged to him. It was like a return, in maturity, to that time of his childhood in Belmont when he had stolen a bicycle and had been arrested. He hadn't stolen an ordinary bicycle. He had stolen a distinctive racing cycle that belonged to a well-known racing cyclist, St Louis; and then, claiming the cycle as his own, a gift from his uncle, he had cycled about Belmont, where St Louis lived.

Trinidad was Malik's manor. Trinidad has a population of just over a million. Much of this population lives in the north-west of the island between the Northern Range and the flat sugar belt, in an urban or a semi-urban sprawl, seemingly unplanned and grabbing, that begins five miles west of Port of Spain and ends about sixteen miles east of the city. Agricultural land is steadily invaded; the hillsides are scratched higher and higher with houses and squatters' shacks and show more

58

brown every year; open spaces, both within the city and outside it, are filled in. The built-up areas choke; the highways are clogged with motorcars; the railway system has been abandoned. Black carrion corbeaux guard the entrance to Port of Spain; and over much of the eastern end of the city, where green hills have been quarried by illegal immigrants from the other islands into dusty red shanty towns, there now hangs the reek of the city's new rubbish dump, burning in the mangrove that once sheltered the scarlet ibis.

It is a 'consumer' squalor. It is not supported by agriculture, which declines, or by industry, which, where it exists, is rudimentary, protected and inflationary. It is supported by what the visitor seldom sees: oil, drilled for in the sea to the north and the south-east, and inland in the south, in forest reserves that are like a country within a country.

Trinidad's urban north-west is a great parasitic suburb, through which money is yet magically cycled. Much of the population is superfluous, and they know it. Unemployment is high but labour is perennially short. The physical squalor, the sense of a land being pillaged rather than built up, generates great tensions; cynicism is like a disease. Race is an irrelevance; but the situation is well suited to the hysteria and evasions of racial politics. And racial politics – preaching oppression and easy redemption, offering only the theory of the enemy, white, brown, yellow, black – have brought the society close to collapse.

Malik, an operator acting always in the racial cause, found in Trinidad his perfect camouflage. He created nothing; but he converted race into money (it didn't matter whose) and success; and that was what many hoped to do. A young 'Black Panther' – connected with a heavily subsidized ninety-acre agricultural cooperative, unproductive because unworked – said admiringly of Malik, even after Malik had fallen: 'He was prime minister of himself and his little group. He was like a little country by himself.' In his year in Trinidad Malik penetrated the society at many points. It was known what he was, but among the cynical and parasitic new men of Trinidad that was like respectability.

He might have risen higher. But then, towards the end of the year, his life took a new twist. Hakim Jamal and Gale Benson arrived from Guyana: Benson, the twenty-seven-year-old English divorcee, in her self-created role as white-woman slave to Jamal's black master, Jamal himself more or less living off a German and anxious about money and his hustling projects. Jamal's line was black schools for the very young and black publishing. He had abandoned his family in California; and he and Benson had been together for about a year, an itinerant hustling team, travelling about the United States in a Volkswagen minibus. They had just been to England to promote Jamal's autobiography; and there they had arranged to come down to Guyana to do a little black business in publishing. Jamal had hoped to take the Guyana government into partnership. But after a month in Guyana he was asked to leave.

Jamal, true American, travelled with his hustler's paraphernalia: life-size printed photographs of himself, brochures of his non-existent Malcolm X Montessori school, and copies of his autobiography. He used the book to introduce himself at Rawle Maximin's garage. He gave Maximin a copy and Maximin told him that Michael X was in Trinidad. 'And it was as though I had told him there was a million dollars under that chair there.' Later Maximin drove Jamal from the Port of Spain Hilton to Arima. 'He asked how far I had got in the book. I said not very far. He took the book and as we were driving he started reading it out. And when he start reading, like he don't want to stop. He spent that night by Michael. In the morning I went to the Hilton and moved down Gale to Arima.'

*

The relationship among these three during November and December 1971 cannot now be known. Jamal used to claim, especially with those white people whom he knew the claim would excite, that he was God; and as God he was Benson's master. But in the Malik commune at Arima, Jamal recognized a more successful outfit and saw its great potential; and Jamal almost immediately decided that Malik was *his* master. He settled in right away, in the house obliquely opposite, which he rented; and soon he was writing a hectoring half-farewell note to a white friend in California, saying that he was through with white people and was for the first time among friends.

Money was short – at the end of November Jamal deposited 500 Trinidad dollars, £104, in a Canadian bank in Port of Spain, and a month later was down to 94 dollars, £19 – but ideas came thick and fast. Jamal's black schools and black publishing merged with Malik's black agriculture into a stupendous black cause. On 10th December Malik wrote to a correspondent in the United States: 'We are now producing reams of literature.' Much of this – copy for the commune – was knocked off by Jamal on the typewriter. Malik was no writer; to Jamal, an American, salesman's prose came naturally. Jamal needed a harbour; Malik depended on other men's ideas. Their talents and roles were complementary; they did not clash.

And it is possible that Gale Benson now became more of an outsider than she had been. She wore African-style clothes that were extravagant even in Trinidad; she had given herself the name of Halé Kimga, an anagram of Gale and Hakim; she went on begging errands for her master. But her cult was of Jamal alone. She didn't appear to be serving the general cause; and she had a way of putting people off. Rawle Maximin found her 'very serious'. When he offered to show her local night-club dances, she said, 'I haven't come here for that.' When she met Lourenço, the Portuguese owner of the stud farm Malik had 'incorporated' into his commune, she spoke to him in Spanish; and Lourenço didn't care for that.

At the same time there was some displeasure in the United States. Jamal, serving Malik and the commune, had been neglecting some of his old associates; and Benson was blamed. It was felt that she possessed him too completely. In December, three weeks before Benson was stabbed to death, an American, writing critically of Benson to some friends in Guyana (and the letter got to Jamal in Trinidad), drew a distinction between Halé Kimga, the devotee, and 'Gailann the secretary'. And that points to something else: Benson's Englishness in spite of her African clothes, and the middle-class manner that seemed at variance with her slave role. 'She was sort of a fake': this was what Malik's wife said later.

Jamal served Malik. But it is possible that he also took him over and gave him a new idea of his role in Trinidad. Jamal dealt in the vehement racial passions of the United States and was obsessed with white people. He didn't understand a place like Trinidad; he didn't understand Malik's position in black and independent Trinidad as 'prime minister of himself and his little group'. He saw it in American terms, as the triumph of a 'nigger'. And so he celebrated it in an eight-page article about Malik (part of the commune literature) which was intended for younger readers – Jamal's first love was black Montessori schools.

He is always giving. You feel bad that there are people who misunderstand him. He teaches, not just by talking, he shows you, for example; he grows orchards [sic]. In his front yard, hanging from his trees there are orchards, dainty flowers that need intense care, but they [yield and deleted] blossom. He grows vegetables for his table and also feeds those passersby who need food ... His chicken farm that feeds thousands of Trinidadians meat. His cows that give milk for babies and for our own health. Then too, there is the stable of horses, thoroughbreds. As he shows them to you, he lectures, but the lecture is real because as he talks about a certain horse, there is the horse. When he speaks of milking cows, you are at the farm, seeing the cows being milked ... You are almost worthy of hearing this man, seeing this man, talking with this man. A man, that England would try to destroy, because they know that somehow this slave, this captured African, had the power of UNDER-STANDING – and what's worse – he understands the slave – he loves the slave – and Brother Michael Abdul Malik, has the nerve, the gall – to be black. Even in a time when he could be anything he wants to be, rich, famous, fashionable, safe – it seems Brother Malik is already too busy being happy as a NIGGER.

A caricature of a caricature; but Jamal, turning Malik into an American, infecting Malik, in the security of Trinidad, with the American-type racial vehemence Malik had so far only parodied, was creating a monster. 'Nigger', success as a kind of racial revenge: these are among the themes of the novel Malik was writing about himself in a cheap lined quarto writing pad, solid un-paragraphed pages in pencil or ballpoint, the writing small, very little crossed out, the number of words noted at the top of each page. At least fifty pages were written; and some of them survived the events they seem so curiously to foreshadow.

The setting is Guyana. A well-appointed house, Malik's, is being described: modern furniture imported from England, fitted carpets, radio phonograph, records, 'a gigantic bookshelf Shakepeare [sic] Shaw Marx Lenin Trotsky Confucius Hugo'. The narrator takes up 'Salammbo that masterpiece of Flaubert's' and finds it dust-free. 'I discover that he not only have the books but actually reads and understands them I was absolutly bowld, litteraly. I took a seat, and gazed upon this marvel, Mike.'

The narrator is a thirty-year-old Englishwoman, Lena Boyd-Richardson. She has been four years in Guyana, doing a bogus job created for her in the firm of Clarkson's by Sir Harold, a friend of her father's; and she is 'really of the opinion these natives are all shifless good for Nothings'. Her house is not far from Michael Malik's, and she often sees 'Mike leaning against the Coconut tree like some statue on a Pedestal, some god, and his little subjects, his little people, Paying Homage to him'. He is in the habit of greeting her in pidgin: 'Like it gwine rain today, mam'; but they do not meet until, for some reason (the early pages are lost), she visits the house. And then 'to top it all he was even talking with a slight Cockney accent to stupify me the more'. He plays some jazz for her on the phonograph, and the 'Thihikosky 1812'; and then the time comes for her to bid 'goodbye to this Amazing man with the Promise to call again'. So the first chapter ends.

Chapter Two is titled 'Run in with Fate'. Lena doesn't call again; but she drives past Mike's house every day and begins to note 'his eyes sometime Mocking and laughing'. She notes his light complexion and wonders about his idling, his shabby clothes, his 'weird double Life'. 'And then again I find myself closing up my doors at night ... the truth I am [afraid *deleted*] scared I am mortally afraid of this man of this Mike the grinning ape, and I can't help liking him, something about him drawing you to him, I wonder how he would look without that Big Beard.'

The run-in with fate follows. Lena, driving through the town one day, nearly runs over a young girl. The girl is Jenny, Mike's eldest daughter, and Lena offers to take her home. Jenny is uneasy, 'scared of what daddy will do if he finds out'; but allows herself to be driven home.

'And there was Mike leaning against the tree as usual with his little retinue around him.' Terror. 'Mike's voice boomed "Jenny come here".' Jenny screams and doesn't move; she is 'shaking too much to say anything sensible'. 'Was it fear?' Lena wonders. 'And if so Fear of what?' Mike's wife, pregnant, runs up 'at a fantastic speed despite her large Stomach'. Mike himself doesn't leave the coconut tree; but 'His Retinue Pulled slightly away from where they were but still not out of earshot.' Jenny is led by her younger sister to Mike. Lena – curiously choosing this moment to observe 'what a great Bond there was' between Jenny and her father – explains that nothing has happened. Mike kisses Jenny, who sobs and says, 'They didn't touch me, daddy.' He walks off towards the house, but the girl still sobs.

'It took me Just one minute to see why the child kept insisting "They didn't touch me", Just a minute to see why she was so scared, and what of. For her father came walking out of the front door as Calm as Ever with a shot gun Under his Arm and Box of shells stuffing some down in his Pocket.' Mike's wife is about to faint, but Lena catches her; and when Mike comes to her, 'she then made a most amazing Transformation, recaptured her poise and said to her husband, "Be Carefull darling, and think first All the time." For someone who did not know the happenings before they could never imagine what this man was going to do. There was that look of finality about him.' Jenny pleads; Lena – 'I too was like if I was dumb' is silent; the wife faints. And Mike walks down the road to the corner.

This is how Lena becomes involved with the family. After some missing pages we find Lena and Mike's wife exchanging memories of England, and Lena hears of Mike's courtship. Nothing, apparently, has happened; tension has been created for its own sake, to prove a point about Mike. Not the least illogical aspect of the scene – with a child screaming, a wife fainting – is the stress on

Mike as family man; but Jamal, in his article about Malik for younger readers, had laid that on with a heavy American hand. A few more pages are missing here; but it is fairly clear that some kind of relationship has developed between Lena and Mike.

And then something extraordinary happens. There is a stumble in the narrative: the writer, without knowing it, suddenly loses his narrator, Lena. In a few connected lines the writer moves from the first-person narrative to third person and then back to first. But now it is Sir Harold, Lena's father's friend, appearing in Guyana, who is the narrator.

Sir Harold comes upon Mike addressing a street-corner meeting in pidgin. Mike's speech is given at length; it is quite incoherent. People must work; but there is nothing wrong with being lazy; Mike himself is lazy and can be seen any day standing in the shade of his tree; he doesn't like to work; but he has worked hard since he was fourteen, and he has worked in England; in England no one pays for the doctor and everything is free, but the taxes are high. The crowd, mixed African and Asian, receives this speech ecstatically. Then Mike, switching from pidgin, says to Sir Harold: 'You come late Sir Harold, I am never at my best when I have my wife waiting.'

Lena, lost for some pages, now reappears. ' "What do you think about him" she asked. I met him once before in England, I said, now I don't know for he seems somehow diffrent. We noticed a movement in the bushes to the side of the house "Dont Pay any attention to that" she said "that Probably some of his Retinue, wherever he is you can be sure there will be some of them hanging around." I felt a Cold wind Pass through me, and decided to go inside.' Mike and his wife prepare to leave. 'Jenny will not sleep if I am not at home,' Mike says. And Sir Harold continues: 'I stood at the door and watched them walk down the Path about 30 seconds after I saw six dark figures slowly follow them "England was never like this" I said to myself and turned inside.'

The pages are now disconnected: 'We could not tear ourselves away from the Presence of this man' – 'the fantastic following he had in the country' – Mike ill with malaria, contracted in Africa when he was young ('never less than two score People standing around the house with a look of anxiety about them': which reads like a borrowed sentence) – Sir Harold offering a job with Clarkson's – shouts in the street: 'We go crown him king.'

An autobiography can distort; facts can be realigned. But fiction never lies: it reveals the writer totally. And Malik's primitive novel is like a pattern book, a guide to later events. That scene of causeless tension at the house with the daughter, the wife, the retinue: just such a scene was witnessed at Arima by a black woman visitor on the Sunday before Joe Skerritt was murdered. 'I can't describe it. I spent just 10 minutes in that house that day. Michael was in the street flying kites. Jennifer wanted some Coke. Her mother said she had to ask her father.' That 'look of finality' that made Lena Boyd Richardson 'like if I was dumb': it was with 'a satanic look', according to Stanley Abbott, that Malik, cutlass in hand and about to murder Skerritt, ordered Abbott: 'I am ready. Bring him.' The political speech in Guyana: even that was to take place, twelve days after the murder of Skerritt. The malaria: that was the excuse Malik gave when, on the run in Guyana, he stayed for three days in his hotel room without drawing the curtains. There remains the mystery of Lena Boyd-Richardson, repelled, fascinated, involved, and then abruptly disappearing as narrator.

So, during November and December 1971, Hakim Jamal and Michael Abdul Malik, in the security of the commune, produced their literature: Jamal, on the typewriter, offering the vision of a triumphant 'nigger', Malik dourly writing his novel in ballpoint and soft pencil, counting each word, awakening old disturbances, arriving at some new definition of himself.

The uneducated Belmont boy had become a man of culture. The London X had become a political hero at home. The man with the silent retinue was the man who in 1965 had told Colin McGlashan of the *Observer*, 'It may sound melodramatic, but there are people who would die for me.' Such a success required witness, English witness; and people like Lena Boyd-Richardson and Sir Harold felt a cold wind of terror. 'England was never like this': Malik, as he wrote, filling the cheap pad, was discovering that he, like his bodyguard and familiar, Steve Yeates, carried the wound of England.

In December, Gale Benson was sent to Guyana to beg for money. To Stanley Abbott, in England, Malik sent a letter with one word: 'Come.' 'Peace and love': that was how the 'brothers' usually signed off in their letters. But the cable from Stanley Abbott that was telephoned to Malik at half-past four on December 10th read like this: ARRIVING 1055 PM SATURDAY 11TH STOP FLIGHT 537 FROM NEW YORK MUCH LOVE TO ALL PEACE AND POWER STANLEY.

From Jamal there went a summons to the United States, to the Negro known as Kidogo, one of his 'co-workers'. Four months before, in London, Jamal had told Jill Tweedie of the *Guardian*: 'If you're going to kill, it must mean something. You should kill people because they are evil, not because they are white.' 'He [Jamal] told me he wanted to send for one of his co-workers,' Malik said in his statement afterwards. 'And just about the same time I noticed through the correspondence I was having from Abbott that he too was coming down to Trinidad.'

So, in December 1971, they began to gather in the two houses of the Arima commune. Simmonds, a white woman who said she had known Malik for ten years, came down from England; and – as she told *The Bomb* afterwards – had 'total involvement' with Steve Yeates, 'an excellent lover ... compassionate ... understanding ... a sense of humour ... a wonderful man'. Kidogo arrived; he didn't stay with Jamal, who knew him, but with Malik, who said he wanted to talk to him about America. Abbott stayed across the road with Jamal. In the third week of December Benson returned from Guyana. She had failed in her begging mission.

On December 31st Steve Yeates, using his Black Muslim name of Muhammed Akbar, went to Cooblal's Hardware and bought a six-inch corner file, charging it to the account of 'Mr Abdhul Mallic, Arima'. Such a file is used in Trinidad for sharpening cutlasses. There was a party at the commune that evening: it was Simmonds's thirtieth birthday. She remembered the food. 'We had bought a calf,' she told *The Bomb*, 'and we had a nice birthday party. A big feed.' Jamal had other memories. He remembered the 'atmosphere of violence' at the commune, and he especially remembered the slaughter of a cow on a neighbouring farm around Christmas time. He told the Boston correspondent of the *Daily Mail* he believed Malik had drunk some of the blood. 'They handed me the cup but I ain't no blood drinker.'

On January 2nd, 1972, Gale Benson was stabbed nine times, one stab going right through the base of her neck. She was buried while still alive in a four-foot hole on the bank of the ravine some two hundred feet north of Malik's house. And she was not missed. Simmonds stayed at the commune until mid-January. Jamal and Kidogo left for the United States on January 20th. Benson's body was not discovered until February 24th. Five men were charged with her murder: an Indian boy called Parmassar, who had attached himself to Malik; a well-to-do Indian of good family called Chadee, who had become mixed up with the commune in December; Malik; Stanley Abbott; and the man called Kidogo, who has still not been found.

*

69

Nineteen seventy-two was a year of rain and floods in Trinidad. Everything was green; bush grew fast. Nineteen seventy-three opened with drought. Every day the hills smoked with scores of separate fires; bamboo clumps ignited; fire, almost colourless in the sunlight, crackled on the roadside verges. The year before the grave of Gale Benson was fresh, hidden from the road by low bush; this year the ravine bank was brown and bare, and the grave was only a shallow hole, dry, crumbling, cleansed by light and heat. During the great days of the commune, Jamal, 'looking out of the glass doors and seeing green, blue and cloud covered mountains', had written to a white correspondent in the United States: 'It is very hot here in the tropics, but it is peaceful, and that is what I both want and need.' Sixteen months after the murder of Benson, Jamal was himself killed, shot on May 2nd, 1973, by a four-man black gang in Boston.

The commune had ended swiftly. Jamal survived it by more than a year. On February 7th, 1972, five weeks after the death of Benson, Joseph Skerritt, a renegade recruit, was brought down to the commune from his mother's house in Belmont. A hole was prepared for him the next morning, and just after midday he was chopped on the neck and buried in the position in which he fell, sprawling, legs apart and slightly raised.

Two days later the commune went on an excursion to Sans Souci bay in the north-east, and Steve Yeates was drowned. A length of bamboo attached to a rope was thrown out to him but he didn't grasp at it. Did he give a grimace of pain before he went under? Or did he grin? Stanley Abbott said: 'Steve gave his life.' So it ended for him, after the thirteen years in England, after the two years of waiting in Trinidad, after the solitary night walks around the Queen's Park Savannah in Port of Spain and the coded messages from the leader in London. After the commune had lasted exactly a year and a day, after the two killings, Muhammed Akbar, Supreme Captain of the Fruit of Islam, Lieutenant Colonel of the Black Liberation Army, was swept out to sea. Nine days later, on February 19th, Malik and his family flew to Guyana. That evening the empty commune house burned down.

The lease had expired on February 9th. Malik, unwilling or unable to exercise his option to buy, had, after a long wrangle with his landlords, received notice to quit. He had gone wild when he had heard, Stanley Abbott said. And to Abbott himself, after the two killings and the drowning of Steve Yeates, the news that Malik didn't own the house, owned nothing, came as a surprise. He felt 'ashamed' and 'deeply hurt'. He had given Malik a book on leadership; and when he saw Malik reading this book, after they had discussed the notice to quit, and after they had discussed their 'needs', Abbott felt like 'going outside for the cutlass' and killing Malik. But then he thought of Malik's children and Malik's pregnant wife.

Abbott told Malik he was tired and needed a rest. Malik gave him a hundred dollars, twenty pounds; and, two days before Malik and his family went to Guyana, Abbott went to Tobago. He stayed with relatives and didn't try to hide. He spent four sleepless nights after he heard that the house had burned down. On February 24th – the body of Gale Benson being disinterred, Malik hiding in a darkened hotel room in Guyana – Abbott flew back to Trinidad. From the airport he took a taxi to Port of Spain. He told the driver to drive slowly. He and the driver talked. He told the driver about the commune. The taxi stopped a little way from police headquarters, and the driver shook Abbott by the hand. Abbott walked to the main entrance of the Victorian Gothic building, spoke to the police sentry at the top of the steps and passed inside. It was a few minutes before midnight.

A year later the Malik house was as the fire had left it. The garden was overgrown, the grass straggly and brown. But the drought had drawn out bright colour from every flowering plant, and bougainvillaea was purple and pink-red on the wire-mesh fence. Beside the peach-coloured hibiscus hedge in the north-west, the hole of Joe Skerritt was dry and cleaned out and shallow, as without drama as that other hole, on the ravine bank. The cover of the septic tank had been dislodged: a dead frog floated. A moraine of litter flowed out from the back door of the house on to the concrete patio between the blackened main house and the untouched servants' quarters. Solidified litter – many burned copies of Malik's autobiography, newspapers and magazines burned and sodden and dried into solid charred cakes. The kitchen was black; the fire was fiercest here. The ceilings everywhere had been burned off and showed the naked corrugated-iron roof, a sheet of which hung down perpendicularly in the living room. All the woodwork was charred. But already a green wild vine, a single long green vine, had run from the overgrown garden on to the gritty terrazzo of the living room.

A murderer can become celebrated and his survival can become a cause. A murdered person can be forgotten. Joe Skerritt was not important, and he is remembered, as a person, only in his mother's house in Belmont. A large unframed pencil portrait is pinned to the wall of the small living room. There are framed photographs of his more successful brother, Anthony (in sea scout uniform), who is in Canada, and of his sister, who was for many years a nurse in England; on a glass cabinet there are the sporting cups won by Michael, another brother. The house is shabby; Mrs Skerritt does lunches for some schoolchildren, but money is short. She looks after her mother, who is senile and shrunken, skin and bones, with thin grey hair tied up tight and sitting on the skull like a coarse knotted handkerchief. Mrs Skerritt ceaselessly relives that morning when Malik came for her son. He called her 'Tantie' and she looked up and saw 'that red man'.

The streets of Belmont are still full of Joe Skerritts.

The walls are still scrawled with the easy threats and easy promises of Black Power. The streets are still full of 'hustlers' and 'scrunters', words that glamourize and seem to give dispensation to those who beg and steal. Another Malik is possible. At every stage of his career he was supported by some kind of jargon and could refer his actions to some kind of revolutionary ideal.

Malik's career proves how much of Black Power – away from its United States source – is jargon, how much a sentimental hoax. In a place like Trinidad, racial redemption is as irrelevant for the Negro as for everybody else. It obscures the problems of a small independent country with a lopsided economy, the problems of a fully 'consumer' society that is yet technologically untrained and without the intellectual means to comprehend the deficiency. It perpetuates the negative, colonial politics of protest. It is, in the end, a deep corruption: a wish to be granted a dispensation from the pains of development, an almost religious conviction that oppression can be turned into an asset, race into money. While the dream of redemption lasts, Negroes will continue to exist only that someone might be their leader. Redemption requires a redeemer; and a redeemer, in these circumstances, cannot but end like the Emperor Jones: contemptuous of the people he leads, and no less a victim, seeking an illusory personal emancipation. In Trinidad, as in every black West Indian island, the too easily awakened sense of oppression and the theory of the enemy point to the desert of Haiti.

Malik, Jamal, Skerritt, Steve Yeates, Stanley Abbott, Benson: they seem purely contemporary, but they played out an old tragedy. If the tragedy of Joe Skerritt and Steve Yeates and Stanley Abbott is contained in O'Neill's 1920 drama of the false redeemer, the tragedy of Gale Benson is contained in an African story of 1897 by Conrad, which curiously complements it: 'An Outpost of Progress', a story of the congruent corruptions of colonizer

73

and colonized, which can also be read as a parable about simple people who think they can separate themselves from the crowd. Benson was as shallow and vain and parasitic as many middle-class dropouts of her time; she became as corrupt as her master; she was part of the corruption by which she was destroyed. And Malik's wife was right. Benson was, more profoundly than Malik or Jamal, a fake. She took, on her journey away from home, the assumptions, however little acknowledged, not only of her class and race and the rich countries to which she belonged, but also of her ultimate security.

Some words from the Conrad story can serve as her epitaph; and as a comment on all those who helped to make Malik, and on those who continue to simplify the world and reduce other men – not only the Negro – to a cause, the people who substitute doctrine for knowledge and irritation for concern, the revolutionaries who visit centres of revolution with return air tickets, the hippies, the people who wish themselves on societies more fragile than their own, all those people who in the end do no more than celebrate their own security.

They were [Conrad wrote] two perfectly insignificant and incapable individuals, whose existence is only rendered possible through the high organization of civilized crowds. Few men realize that their life, the very essence of their character, their capabilities and audacities, are only the expression of their belief in the safety of their surroundings. The courage, the composure, the confidence; the emotions and principles; every great and every insignificant thought belongs not to the individual but to the crowd: to the crowd that believes blindly in the irresistible force of its institutions and of its morals, in the power of its police and of its opinion.

One of the last letters Benson received was from her father, Captain Leonard Plugge, who lived in California but continued to use writing paper headed with his Belgravia address. With this letter Captain Plugge sent a translation he had done — typed out on the Belgravia paper and photocopied — of some lines by Lamartine:

On these white pages, where my verses unfold,
May oft a souvenir, perchance your heart recall.
Your life also only pure white pages behold,
With one word, happiness, I would cover them all.
But the book of life is a volume all sublime,
That we cannot open, or close just at our time,
On the page where one loves, one would wish to linger,
Yet the page where one dies, hides beneath the finger.

March–July 1973

4   Postscript

Abbott was given twenty years for the murder of Joe Skerritt. Malik was sentenced to death by hanging. Both Malik and Abbott appealed against their sentences. And it was only after their appeals had been dismissed — and after the above account had been written — that the trial for the Gale Benson murder took place.

Five men were accused of the murder. But only two were actually tried: Abbott again, and an Indian motor-car salesman named Chadee, who had been hoping to sell twelve cars to Malik and had then become mixed up with the Malik group. Three of the accused couldn't be tried. Steve Yeates was dead, drowned at Sans Souci, his body never recovered; Kidogo, Jamal's American 'co-worker', was in the United States and couldn't be found; Malik was already under sentence of death. So Malik was never tried for the murder of Benson. It was Abbott who had to go through the calvary of two murder trials.

The murder of Benson was decided on by both Malik

and Jamal. It was at the time when the two men were working on one another and exciting one another and producing 'reams of literature'. Jamal was writing his exalted, off-the-mark 'nigger' nonsense about Malik; and Malik, in his novel, with this Jamal-given idea of his power (and no longer a man on the run, as in his previous fiction), was settling scores with the English middle class, turning the fascination of 'Sir Harold' and 'Lena Boyd-Richardson' into terror.

This was a literary murder, if ever there was one. Writing led both men there: for both of them, uneducated but clever, hustlers with the black cause always to hand, operating always among the converted or half-converted, writing had for too long been a public relations exercise, a form of applauded lie, fantasy. And in Arima it was a fantasy of power that led both men to contemplate, from their different standpoints, the act of murder. Jamal, when he understood that Trinidad wasn't the United States, began to feel that in an island where the majority of the population was black, he didn't 'look good' with a white woman at his side. And Benson, English and middle class, was just the victim Malik needed: his novel began to come to life.

Malik summoned Abbott from London. He sent a one-word letter: 'Come.' And Abbott took the first flight out, travelling first to New York and then down to Trinidad. Malik and Steve Yeates met him at the airport and drove him the few miles to the Malik house in Christina Gardens in Arima. Malik's wife was there; the Malik children were asleep. And there Abbott met Jamal for the first time. Later Abbott was taken across the road to the other house, the one Jamal and Benson were renting; it was where he was to stay. Abbott didn't see Benson there; she had gone to Guyana to try to raise money for Jamal, but was going to be back in a few days. (Benson's movements at this time are not absolutely clear. Her papers were destroyed the day she was killed.)

The four men – Abbott, Malik, Steve Yeates and Jamal – talked through the night. At one stage Abbott asked about The People's Store. This was Malik's first Black Power 'commune' project in Trinidad; and Abbott had earlier in the year worked on it for a month, helping with the painting and the polishing. Abbott said he wanted to see what the place looked like, and the four men drove the twenty miles or so to Carenage, where the store was.

While they drove – in the Sunday-morning darkness – Malik said they now had the best working group in the universe, that they were going places, and were the chosen ones. Abbott thought that Malik was talking to impress Jamal. 'With Jamal,' Abbott said, 'he kept on with this mind-destroying talk.' And Abbott was disappointed by what he saw of the Carenage house, on which he and Yeates and others had worked so hard just a few months before. 'I saw the house and saw three men – Negroes – living there. I said the house was dirty and it appeared the men were neglected. It looked as though Michael had just placed these men there and neglected them.' They drove back to Arima and Christina Gardens. It was now light; and as though to make up for the Carenage disappointment, Malik showed Abbott the improvements he had made in the Arima house and yard.

The men at Carenage had looked neglected. And that was how Abbott soon began to feel. After the drama of the urgent summons to Trinidad, it seemed that there was nothing important for him to do. He was made to do various yard jobs. He cut bamboo grass for the goats Malik kept and made long journeys to get the hibiscus Malik said the goats needed; he mowed the lawn; he washed the car and the jeep; and he was sent out by Malik to work without payment on the farm that supplied a gallon of milk a day to the Malik family and commune. Abbott said he wanted to be released, to go and live at his mother's. Malik refused.

It was Malik's custom to wake Abbott up at seven in

the morning. One morning – two days before Christmas, and less than a fortnight after he had arrived – Abbott saw blood on Malik's mouth and beard. 'I told him his mouth was bleeding. What had happened? He said they had killed a calf on the Lourenço farm that morning, and he was drinking blood. I felt scared and sick.' And there was soon another reason for fear. 'I heard him speak to Hakim Jamal before the Christmas. He told him to send for somebody in the United States whom he, Jamal, could trust. At that point I walked off, because they were not talking to me. A couple days later this American man, Kidogo, arrived. I again beseeched Michael to allow me to go home, now that he had someone else around to help him. He told me Kidogo was not there for manual work. He told me Kidogo was a hired killer. He elaborated that Kidogo had killed police and all sorts in Boston in the United States, and for me to shut up from now on.'

Kidogo, as an American, didn't need a visa. And in Christina Gardens he swanned around, a Bostonian among the natives, taking a lot of photographs with an Instamatic camera, helping with none of the household or menial chores, apparently saving himself for his special job. He bought a cutlass and fooled around with it in the yard; in his idleness he carved the letter K on the wooden haft.

If Abbot was afraid of Kidogo because he thought of Kidogo as a professional, there were people in the commune who were just as afraid of Abbott. One day, when Abbott was washing the jeep, Malik said to Chadee, the motorcar salesman, 'That man is a psychopath.' Chadee never trusted Abbott after that. This was how, in the commune, Malik orchestrated fear and kept everyone in his retinue up to mark.

Benson returned from Guyana, and it was full house at the commune on Christmas Day. Abbott would have liked to visit his mother that day, but he wasn't allowed to go. He stayed with the others; and in his statement afterwards he spoke of the Christmas gathering at Christina Gardens with an odd formality, an odd deference to the women of the two houses. 'We all spent Christmas together, including Mrs Michael, her children, and Jamal's lady, Halé, who was an Englishwoman whom I met at Michael's house.' There were two other English people: a man called Granger, and the woman called Simmonds, then in 'total involvement' with Steve Yeates.

On December 31st, Yeates, Simmonds's 'excellent lover', found time to buy a six-inch file. And it must have been that file Abbott saw Kidogo using – that very day, or the day after – on the cutlass on whose haft he had carved the letter K. Kidogo's cutlass was a 'gilpin'. The blade of the gilpin widens at the end and curves backward to a sharp point, like a scimitar. Abbott saw Kidogo filing off 'the gilpin part' of the cutlass and asked him why. Kidogo – a professional, but clearly inexperienced with cutlasses – said it didn't 'balance properly'.

In the evening there was a party: Old Year's Night, and it was also Simmonds's thirtieth birthday. They ate the calf that had been killed eight days before; and Simmonds enjoyed the 'big feed'.

Malik had invited Chadee, the motorcar salesman, to the Old Year's Night party. Chadee, a man of thirty, of a goodish Indian family but of no great personal attainments (he was also a part-time debt collector), thought that Malik was very rich. At their first meeting, a few months before, Malik had said he wanted to buy twelve new cars, and Chadee was hoping to do big business with Malik. Malik saw Chadee as a man with many interesting contacts, a possible commune recruit, and he had begun to involve Chadee in the Commune's social occasions. Two or three weeks before the calf feast, Chadee had been taken by Malik on a moonlight beach picnic.

And now, just after midday on New Year's Day, Chadee came again to Christina Gardens. He called first on Jamal and Benson. Chadee had been introduced to them a month or so before by Malik; and Malik had told Chadee at the time that Jamal didn't really like Benson, that Jamal didn't think he looked 'good' with a white woman in Trinidad. Chadee now wished Benson and Jamal a happy new year; and Benson, who apparently didn't have too much to say to Chadee, then left the two men together. They sat out in the veranda. Jamal, still besotted by his own writing, read out passages from his autobiography to Chadee, in all the heat of the early tropical afternoon, and spoke of the book he was writing about Malik.

Later Chadee went across the road to Malik's and wished Malik a happy new year. He saw Abbott. Abbott had been given permission to visit his mother that day, and Abbott asked Chadee to drive him there (Malik never lent his vehicles). Chadee agreed; and he and Abbott decided to take along Parmassar, an Indian boy who was glamoured by Malik and was a member of Malik's group. They drove to Montrose Village, to Abbott's mother's house. Abbott's mother was a retired schoolteacher, seventy-one years old. Abbott was proud of her and Chadee found her 'a pleasant, charming person; she was articulate and expressed herself well'. The three men were given cake and ginger ale. They left at seven, and it was about half-past seven when they got back to Malik's house in Christina Gardens. Malik asked Chadee to drive his car into the yard. When Chadee did so, the gate was closed. Malik then asked Chadee to hang around with the boys for a while, and Chadee hung around.

At a quarter to nine – and at this stage everything appears to follow a timetable – Malik told the men present that he wanted to talk to them privately in the servants' quarters at the back of his house. One of Malik's daughters was there, listening to records with a black girl who did occasional secretarial work for Malik. Malik told the two girls to go elsewhere. There were cushions on the floor; Malik asked the men to sit. Malik himself sat on a chair. Steve Yeates sat on a cushion on Malik's right, Kidogo on a cushion on Malik's left. Facing them, and sitting on cushions, were the boy Parmassar, Chadee and Abbott. Jamal was not there.

Malik said that Jamal was suffering from mental strain, that Benson was the cause of the strain, and that she had to be got rid of. Abbott said Malik could give her a plane ticket and let her go back where she came from. At this, Yeates – the man with the wound of England on his back – jumped up and said he wanted 'something definite'. 'Michael just sat stroking his beard,' Abbott said, 'and said he wanted blood.' Blood was the only thing that could keep them together.

Kidogo said nothing. He just looked at Abbott and Abbott saw murder in Kidogo's eyes, and Yeates's, and Malik's. Abbott didn't look at Parmassar or at Chadee. And Chadee was sick with fear. Malik had told him that Abbott was a psychopath, and Chadee felt now that it was true. He didn't believe what Abbott had said about giving Benson a plane ticket. He thought it was said to trap him into making a statement that would turn them all against him. So Chadee said nothing, and Malik outlined his plan.

In the morning they would dig a hole for Benson, by the manure heap at the dead end of the road. Steve Yeates would take Benson to the farm to get milk and keep her looking at the cows while the hole was being dug; Malik would take Jamal to some other place, take him out for an early-morning drive. The hole would have to be dug fast, in forty-five minutes. That was all that was said then by Malik: a hole was to be dug in a certain place, within a certain time, for a certain purpose. Steve Yeates was to bring Benson to the hole; but nothing was said about how Benson was to be killed, or who was to kill her. And nobody asked. As for Chadee, he wasn't to go home. He and the other Indian, the boy Parmassar, were to sleep in that room, on the cushions. And, Malik said, everybody should go to sleep early and get up before the sun. At ten o'clock the meeting was over.

Abbott left to go across the road to Jamal's house, where he had his room. Malik reminded Abbott to lock the gate as he left the yard; and Chadee saw in that instruction about the gate a direct threat to himself, a further order to stay where he was. Malik, after this, got up and went to the main house. Chadee didn't see what he could do. The boy Parmassar was with him; Steve Yeates was in the second bedroom of the servants' quarters; Kidogo had the back bedroom in the main house, just across the patio from the servants' quarters. Chadee lay down on the cushions next to Parmassar. His mind was 'in a mess'; he had never heard 'such a conversation' before. He prayed to God and hoped that in the morning the plan would be forgotten. Then his mind went blank and he fell asleep.

Across the road, in the house with Jamal and Benson, Abbott didn't sleep. He was lying down in his clothes, thinking. He thought about his mother and what Malik might do to her. He remembered the looks Malik, Kidogo and Steve Yeates had given him earlier in the evening.

At six in the morning Malik woke Parmassar. Parmassar woke Chadee, sleeping beside him on the cushions. And then Malik sent Parmassar across the road to get Abbott, to tell him that the time had come to start digging the hole for Benson. Parmassar didn't have to wake Abbott: Abbott hadn't slept, and was still in his clothes.

They were all up now. Chadee saw Steve Yeates and Kidogo come out of Kidogo's room. Yeates called Chadee out into the yard, and Chadee sat outside against the kitchen of the main house. Kidogo and Parmassar (reappearing) went 'to the back' and began to collect tools: a spade, a fork, two shovels, a cutlass and a file. They asked Chadee to help. He took the two shovels. Parmassar had the fork and the spade; Kidogo had the cutlass and the file. Abbott was waiting outside the gate. They passed the tools to him, climbed over the gate and walked down the road to the dead end, two hundred feet away from the house, on waste ground above the ravine.

Not long afterwards Malik reversed his Humber car to where the four men were – Abbott, Kidogo, Parmassar and Chadee – and showed them where the hole was to be dug. It was beside a manure heap; Chadee saw 'a lot of bamboo poles around the manure'. Malik asked Kidogo for the time. Kidogo said it was six-twenty, and Malik said again that they had forty-five minutes to dig the hole. Malik himself wasn't going to be present while anything happened. As he had said the previous evening, he was going to take Jamal out for a drive, to keep Jamal out of the way. And it was only now – sitting in his car – that he gave his final orders. Not to all of them, but only to Abbott. He called Abbott over to the car.

Abbott went and said, 'Oh, God, Michael, you don't have to do this. Spare the woman.' Malik said he didn't want to hear any more of 'that old talk from last night'. 'He sat behind the wheel pulling his beard and watching me. He told me that Steve Yeates would drive up in the jeep; he will bring the woman Halé out. I was to tell her when she saw the hole, if she got suspicious, that it was for stuff to be decomposed, or words to that effect. He told me I was to grab that woman and take her into the hole. When I had her I was to tell her what the hole was for: to tell her it was for Jamal.' As for the killing itself, that was to be done by Kidogo. 'He told me Kidogo had his orders. He said that if I did anything to endanger the safety of the men around that hole, or his family or himself, by not obeying, I would die. What he was telling me was I would die that morning with the knowledge that my mother would be dead also, because that was where he was heading with Jamal.' Abbott prepared to obey. 'He also told me, as I was walking off, to remind Kidogo that the heart is on the left side. He wants the heart.'

Malik drove away, and Abbott passed on his instructions: Kidogo was to do the killing, and Kidogo had to remember that the heart was below the left breast. The four men began to dig furiously. Kidogo was in charge, and he told them to burn themselves up, one man digging at a time, as hard and as fast as he could, until he could dig no more. Chadee, the salesman, suffered; Abbott helped him. It was Abbott, in fact, in his particular frenzy, who did most of the digging. When they had been digging for some time, Steve Yeates came with the jeep. He was about to take Benson to the farm, and he wanted a watch. Chadee lent him his; and Kidogo and Steve Yeates synchronized the watches before Steve Yeates left.

When the hole, which was about four feet square, was four feet deep, Kidogo said they had dug enough. Kidogo rested. He gave his cutlass to the boy Parmassar and asked Parmassar to sharpen it. Parmassar sharpened the cutlass and gave it back to Kidogo.

At seven-fifteen the jeep came reversing down the road. Steve Yeates was driving, and Benson was with him. The jeep stopped; Yeates got out and told Benson to come out, too, and see how hard the boys had been working. She got out of the jeep. She was in a light African-style gown; the boy Parmassar remembered that it had short sleeves. She said, 'Good morning,' and the men around the hole said, 'Good morning.'

Abbott said, 'Come and see what we are doing.' She walked nearer the hole. She said, 'What is it for?' Abbott said, 'It is to put fresh matter to be decomposed. Come and look. Do you like it?' She said, 'Yes. But why?' Abbott didn't say, 'It is for Jamal.' He forgot that. He said, 'It is for you.' He held his right hand over her mouth, twisted her left hand behind her with his left hand, and jumped with her into the shallow hole. Kidogo jumped in at once with his sharpened cutlass and began to use it on her, cutting through the African gown, aiming at the heart. She fought back hard; she kicked. She called out to Steve Yeates, 'Steve, Steve, what have I done to deserve this?' He remained leaning against the jeep, watching.

And Kidogo, after all, didn't know how to use a cutlass to kill. He jut slashed and stabbed, inflicting superficial cuts; and Benson was asking him why, speaking 'intimately' to him, as it sounded to Abbott, who was struggling to hold the frantic woman. Abbott's own thoughts were far away. He was thinking of his mother: she would ask Malik and Jamal in, when they got to the house in Montrose Village, and they just had to tell her that he, Abbott, was ill, and she would get into Malik's car and be brought to Arima. Kidogo was still using the cutlass on Benson. He was like a madman, and with the three of them in that small hole Abbott began to fear that he might himself be killed. In his panic and confusion he called out, stupidly, 'Somebody help! Somebody do something!' And when Chadee looked he saw a great cut on the left elbow Benson had raised to protect herself against Kidogo's cutlass. It was her first serious wound.

Steve Yeates, still beside the jeep, looked at Chadee and at Parmassar. Then he went to the hole and took away the cutlass from Kidogo. There were now four of them in the hole. But Yeates didn't need much room. With his left-hand he placed the sharpened point of the cutlass at the base of Benson's throat; with his right hand he hit the haft hard. It was a simple, lucid action, the most lucid since Abbott had taken Benson into the hole; but of all the men there Yeates was the one with the purest hate. The broad blade went in six inches, and Benson made a gurgling noise. She fell and began to 'beat about' in the hole. Yeates and Kidogo and Abbott got out of the hole. It would have been about seven-thirty.

Kidogo called, 'Cover!' Benson's feet were still beating about. Chadee began to pull manure from the manure heap into the hole. Yeates, lucid as ever, stopped Chadee. It would look strange if the manure heap was disturbed, he said. Better to go to the farm and get a fresh load. He and Yeates went in the jeep. When they came back they found Benson already buried in her hole, and they dumped the manure to one side.

They all went back then to the Malik house. Chadee

went to the kitchen and drank a glass of water. Yeates parked the jeep. Kidogo cleaned his cutlass. Parmassar and Abbott sat side by side on the kitchen steps.

The telephone in the kitchen rang. It didn't awaken Malik's wife or children. Chadee answered the phone. It was Malik, telephoning from Abbott's mother's house. Was everything all right? Malik asked. Chadee said yes. When Yeates, coming in just then, asked about the telephone, and Chadee told him, Yeates 'blew' – he gave, that is, a sigh of relief. It was eight o'clock.

At half-past eight Malik came back with Jamal. Malik said, 'Is the tree planted?' Agriculture, the commune, the life of labour: Malik always had his own coded way with language. Abbott wasn't sure if anyone answered. Malik asked how deep the hole was, and everyone gave a different depth. He said they should put on a couple of loads of manure.

Agricultural conversation: that was all that Jamal could say he had heard, after his morning's drive to Abbott's mother's house, and his cup of coffee with the old lady. Because it had apparently been decided that Jamal should be involved in no way. Jamal had to see nothing and hear nothing; and had to be able to say that Benson had just gone away, taking her things. That remained to be done: getting rid of Benson's things. And Jamal was not to see; and the two English visitors at the commune were not to see or suspect; and Malik's wife and two daughters, and Malik's secretarial assistant, who was coming in that morning. Everyone had to see only another busy commune day.

It had been planned in detail. There were seven men in all (leaving out the English visitor), and their movements that morning and afternoon had been plotted in advance. Malik, after that agricultural conversation, announced a commune building job. They were going to Parmassar's mother's house, to help the poor lady rebuild her kitchen. It wasn't far away. Abbott, Kidogo, Chadee,

Yeates and Parmassar himself were sent ahead in the jeep. Malik and Jamal came later. They broke down the old kitchen and sketched out a plan for the new one. But they didn't have cement and sand. Malik sent Chadee and Kidogo in the jeep back to Christina Gardens, to get sand and a bag of cement from his yard – it was a day of movement like this, movement and camouflage.

When they got to Malik's yard, Kidogo disappeared, leaving Chadee to load the cement and sand by himself. Chadee loaded up, and looked for Kidogo. He couldn't find him. It was one of Malik's daughters who told Chadee that Kidogo was in Jamal's house across the road. Chadee went to the house – where less than twenty-four hours before he had wished Benson a happy new year – and found Kidogo in Jamal's and Benson's bedroom.

Kidogo – doing his job – was packing Benson's clothes and papers. He had already packed one bag and wrapped it in cloth; he was packing a second. He told Chadee to bring the jeep round. When Chadee went to Malik's yard to get the jeep, he had a little fright. Malik's secretarial assistant asked for a lift to the Arima taxi stand. Chadee explained about the sand and cement and said he would send Steve Yeates to give her a lift; and the girl didn't insist. He took the jeep round to Jamal's and Kidogo threw in the bags with Benson's things.

Malik was waiting for them at Parmassar's mother's house. Chadee reversed the jeep right into the yard, and Malik and Kidogo took the bags and put them in the boot of Malik's car. The sand and cement were unloaded, and concrete was mixed for the new kitchen. Parmassar's mother and sisters had prepared lunch for the working party. But Chadee didn't eat; he just had some fruit juice. When he came out of the house after the lunch he saw that somebody had put some dry wood in the jeep. And then Malik and Yeates took the bags with Benson's things from the boot of Malik's car and put them back in the jeep.

Chadee, Abbott and Kidogo were told to go in the jeep with Yeates. As they drove off, Yeates said they were going 'up the river' to burn Benson's clothes. They stopped at a filling station in Arima and bought some kerosene, and they drove eight miles to Guanapo Heights, beside the Guanapo River. Yeates left the three men there, with the wood and kerosene and the bags. And he gave them a message from Malik: they were to keep the fire burning, because in an hour's time Malik and his children were coming to the river to bathe.

Chadee stood guard while Abbott and Kidogo got a fire going on the riverbank with the wood and the kerosene. They burned Benson's clothes and papers piece by piece. Certain things couldn't be burned. Chadee buried these a short distance away, digging a hole two feet deep. There was less of a rush now than in the morning, and the digging came more easily to him. Kidogo and Abbott left Chadee for a while; and Chadee, doing as he had been told, looked for more wood and kept the fire going. When Kidogo and Abbott came back they were carrying fruit in one of the bags into which Benson's things had been stuffed earlier: it was an extra precautionary touch.

Shortly afterwards, keeping strict time, Steve Yeates drove up with the jeep, and he had brought a whole party: Malik, Malik's two daughters, Jamal, and the young Englishman who was a guest in the commune. They all bathed in the river, and then they warmed themselves at the fire. No one asked about the fire. Malik didn't ask Abbott or Kidogo or Chadee any questions.

Blood in the morning, fire in the afternoon. But to an observer who wasn't looking for special clues, to someone on the outside seeing only the busyness with car and jeep and sand and cement, it would only have been a good commune day: constructive work in the morning, and then a bathing party in a tropical wood.

That bathing party, with the fire on the riverbank: it was the crowning conception of an intricate day. Like an episode in a dense novel, it served many purposes and had many meanings. And it had been devised by a man who was writing a novel about himself, settling accounts with the world, filling pages of the cheap writing pad and counting the precious words as he wrote, anxious for world fame (including literary fame): a man led to lunacy by all the ideas he had been given of who he was, and now, in the exile of Arima, under the influence of Jamal, with an illusion of achieved power. Malik had no skills as a novelist, not even an elementary gift of language. He was too self-absorbed to process experience in any rational way or even to construct a connected narrative. But when he transferred his fantasy to real life, he went to work like the kind of novelist he would have liked to be.

Such plotting, such symbolism! The blood of the calf at Christmas time, the blood of Gale Benson in the new year. And then, at the end of the sacrificial day, the cleansing in the river, with Benson's surrogate pyre on the bank. So many other details: so many things had had to be worked out. Neither Chadee nor Abbott (with their special anxieties) had been left alone for any length of time during the day; both men had always been under the eye of Kidogo or Steve Yeates. And Jamal had always been sheltered. He had been at Abbott's mother's house while Benson was being killed and buried; and he had been at Parmassar's mother's house, helping with the kitchen, when Kidogo was clearing away Benson's clothes and papers from the bedroom that had been hers and Jamal's.

It had been thought out over many weeks. And it worked. Benson had always been withdrawn, and now she was not missed. For a fortnight or more everybody in the two houses at Christina Gardens stayed together. The two English visitors remained, the woman Simmonds continuing in her 'total involvement' with Steve Yeates; towards the end there was even some talk of a restaurant that she and Yeates might run together.

Chadee didn't go home. On the evening of the murder

Malik told him that he and Parmassar, the two Indians in the group, had become 'members for life'; and that night, after he had gone with Steve Yeates to fetch his clothes, Chadee slept again in the bedroom of the servants' quarters in Malik's house. Later he was given a room in Jamal's house, and he began to mow the lawn and do other yard jobs.

But then the commune Christmas party began to break up. The two English visitors went away. And – eighteen days after the murder – Jamal and Kidogo went away, back to Boston. Jamal acknowledged Malik as the master, and Malik thought of himself as the master. But Malik had grown to need Jamal more than he knew. Without Jamal's own lunacy, his exaltation, his way with words, his vision of the master, Malik's fantasies of power grew wilder and unfocused, without art, the rages of a gangster. He thought of kidnapping the wife of a bank manager; he ordered Abbott to plan the 'liquidation' of a family. And then, for no reason except that of blood, and because he was now used to the idea of killing with a cutlass, he killed Joseph Skerritt.

It was the murder of Skerritt that finally unhinged Steve Yeates, 'Muhammed Akbar', Supreme Captain of the Fruit of Islam. Yeates dealt in racial hate; he was pure in his hate; and he couldn't understand why Skerritt had been killed. Every time he looked through his window he saw Skerritt's grave; and the fast that Malik ordered after the killing of Skerritt didn't help. They were all weakened and perhaps made a little light-headed by four days of fasting when they went on the excursion to the dangerous bay of Sans Souci; and Yeates, when he got into trouble with the strong currents, seemed at a certain moment to have decided not to listen to the shouts of people anxious to save him, not to struggle, to surrender. Abbott thought that Yeates drowned himself; and Abbott thought that before he went down Yeates gave a final wave with his left hand.

That was the beginning of the end of the commune. Blood didn't keep them together for long. Abbott helped Chadee and Parmassar to escape; Abbott himself went to Tobago; Malik went to Guyana, and the house in Christina Gardens burned down.

Fifty-five days after the killing of Benson, Chadee took a police inspector to Guanapo Heights and showed where he had buried those things of Benson's that couldn't be burned. This was the police inventory, which Chadee certified:

One brown leather sleeveless jacket; one brown leather hippy bag; one pair of lady's pink mod boots; one pair of brown shoes; one pair of brown slippers; three silver bracelets; one empty small bottle; one tube Avon Rose-mint cream; one tube of Tangee cream; one small circular face mirror; a quantity of black wool; two hippy pendants; one tin containing Flapyl tablets; one small scissors; one plastic rule; one triangular keyholder; one empty Limacol bottle; one brown small tablespoon; one Liberation of Jerusalem medallion with 7.6.1967 stamped thereon; one brown belt with a buckle made in the form of a heart; one damaged grey suitcase; one large scissors; one blue ballpoint pen; one damaged brown suitcase; one silver ring with the Star of David; and one gold ring with two stones.

Malik appealed many times against the death sentence. And it was only when legal arguments were exhausted, and the appeal was on the grounds of cruelty – on the grounds that, after the long delay, the carrying out of the death sentence would be an act of cruelty – it was only then that the point was made that Malik was mad. The point, if it had been made at the beginning, might have saved Malik's life. But, for too many people in London and elsewhere, Malik had embodied, at one and the same time, the vicious black man and the good black cause. A plea of insanity would have made nonsense of a whole school of theatre; and among the people abroad who supported Malik there were those who continued to see his conviction for murder as an act of racial and political persecution. So Malik played out to the end the role that had been given him.

He was hanged in the Royal Gaol in central Port of Spain in May 1975, three years and four months after the killing of Benson. His wife sat in a square nearby. There was a small silent crowd with her in the square, waiting for the sound of the trap door at eight, hanging time. The body of the hanged man was taken in a coffin to the Golden Grove Prison, not far from Arima; and there bare-backed prisoners in shorts carried the coffin to its grave in the prison grounds.

Chadee was sentenced to death, but this was later commuted to life imprisonment. Abbott, after his twenty years for the murder of Skerritt, was sentenced to death for his part in the murder of Benson. His was the true agony: he rotted for nearly six years in a death cell, and was hanged only in April 1979. He never became known outside Trinidad, this small, muscular man with the straight back, the soldierly demeanour, the very pale skin, and the underslept tormented eyes. He was not the X; he became nobody's cause; and by the time he was hanged, that caravan had gone by.

The Return of Eva Perón

1 The Corpse at the Iron Gate

Buenos Aires, April–June 1972

Outline it like a story by Borges.

The dictator is overthrown and more than half the people rejoice. The dictator had filled the gaols and emptied the treasury. Like many dictators, he hadn't begun badly. He had wanted to make his country great. But he wasn't himself a great man; and perhaps the country couldn't be made great. Seventeen years pass. The country is still without great men; the treasury is still empty; and the people are on the verge of despair. They begin to remember that the dictator had a vision of the country's greatness, and that he was a strong man: they begin to remember that he had given much to the poor. The dictator is in exile. The people begin to agitate for his return. The dictator is now very old. But the people also remember the dictator's wife. She loved the poor and hated the rich, and she was young and beautiful. So she has remained, because she died young, in the middle of the dictatorship. And, miraculously, her body has not decomposed.

'That,' Borges said, 'is a story I could *never* write.'

But at seventy-six, and after seventeen years of proscription and exile, Juan Perón, from the Madrid suburb known as the Iron Gate, dictates peace terms to the military regime of Argentina. In 1943, as an army colonel preaching a fierce nationalism, Perón became a power in Argentina; and from 1946 to 1955, through two election victories, he ruled as dictator. His wife Eva held no official position, but she ruled with Perón until 1952. In that year she died. She was expensively embalmed, and now her corpse is with Perón at the Iron Gate.

In 1956, just one year after his overthrow by the army, Perón wrote from Panama, 'My anxiety was that some clever man would have taken over.' Now, after eight presidents, six of them military men, Argentina is in a state of crisis that no Argentine can fully explain. The mighty country, as big as India and with a population of twenty-three million, rich in cattle and grain, Patagonian oil, and all the mineral wealth of the Andes, inexplicably drifts. Everyone is disaffected. And suddenly nearly everyone is Peronist. Not only the workers, on whom in the early days Perón showered largesse, but Marxists and even the middle-class young, whose parents remember Perón as a tyrant, torturer and thief.

The peso has gone to hell: from 5 to the dollar in 1947, to 16 in 1949, 250 in 1966, 400 in 1970, 420 in June last year, 960 in April this year, 1,100 in May. Inflation, which has been running at a steady 25 per cent since the Perón days, has now jumped to 60 per cent. The banks are offering 24 per cent interest. Inflation, when it reaches this stage of takeoff, is good only for the fire insurance business. Premiums rise and claims fall. When prices gallop away week by week, fires somehow do not often get started.

For everyone else it is a nightmare. It is almost impossible to put together capital; and even then, if you are thinking of buying a flat, a delay of a week can cost you two or three hundred U.S. dollars (many business people prefer to deal in dollars). Salaries, prices, the exchange rate: everyone talks money, everyone who can afford it buys dollars on the black market. And soon even the visitor is touched by the hysteria. In two months a hotel room rises from 7,000 pesos to 9,000, a tin of tobacco from 630 to 820. Money has to be changed in small amounts; the market has to be watched. The peso drops one day to 1,250 to the dollar. Is this a freak, or the beginning of a new decline? To hesitate that day was to lose: the peso bounced back to 1,100. 'You begin to feel,' says Norman Thomas di Giovanni, the translator of Borges, who has come to the end of his three-year stint in Buenos Aires, 'that you are spending the best years of your life at the moneychanger's. I go there some afternoons the way other people go shopping. Just to see what's being offered.'

The blanket wage rises that the government decrees from time to time – 15 per cent in May, and another 15 per cent promised soon – cannot keep pace with prices. 'We've got to the stage,' the ambassador's wife says, 'when we can calculate the time between the increase in wages and the increase in prices.' People take a second job and sometimes a third. Everyone is obsessed with the need to make more money and at the same time to spend quickly. People gamble. Even in the conservative Andean town of Mendoza the casino is full; the patrons are mainly workpeople, whose average monthly wage is the equivalent of fifty dollars. The queues that form all over Buenos Aires on a Thursday are of people waiting to hand in their football-pool coupons. The announcement of the pool results is a weekly national event.

A spectacular win of some 330 million pesos by a Paraguayan labourer dissipated a political crisis in mid-April. There had been riots in Mendoza, and the army had been put to flight. Then, in the following week, a guerrilla group in Buenos Aires killed the Fiat manager whom they had kidnapped ten days earlier. On the same day, in the nearby industrial town of Rosario, guerrillas ambushed and killed General Sánchez, commander of the Second Army Corps, who had some reputation as a torturer. Blood called for blood: there were elements in the armed forces that wanted then to break off the negotiations with Perón and scotch the elections promised next year. But the Paraguayan's fortune lengthened all conversation, revived optimism and calmed nerves. The little crisis passed.

The guerrillas still raid and rob and blow up; they still occasionally kidnap and occasionally kill. The guerrillas are young and middle class. Some are Peronist, some are communist. After all the bank raids the various organizations are rich. In Córdoba last year, according to my information, a student who joined the Peronist Montoneros was paid the equivalent of 70 dollars a month; lawyers were retained at 350 dollars. 'You could detect the young Montoneros by their motorcars, their aggressiveness, their flashiness. James Dean types. Very glamorous.' Another independent witness says of the guerrillas he has met in Buenos Aires: 'They're anti-American. But one of them held a high job in an American company. They have split personalities; some of them really don't know who they are. They see themselves as a kind of comic-book hero. Clark Kent in the office by day, Superman at night, with a gun.'

Once you make a decision [the thirty-year-old woman says] you feel better. Most of my friends are for the revolution and they feel much better. But sometimes they are like children who can't see too much of the future. The other day I went with my friend to the cinema. He is about thirty-three. We went to see *Sacco and Vanzetti*. At the end he said, 'I feel ashamed not being a *guerrillero*. I feel I am an accomplice of this government, this way of life.' I said, 'But you lack the violence. A *guerrillero* must be *despejado* – he mustn't have too much imagination or sensibility. You have to do as you are told. If not, nothing comes out well. It is like a religion, a dogma.' And again he said, 'Don't you feel *ashamed?*'

The film maker says:

I think that after Marx people are very conscious of history. The decay of colonialism, the emergence of the Third World – they see themselves acting out some role in this process. This is as dangerous as having no view of history at all. It makes people very vain. They live in a kind of intellectual cocoon. Take away the jargon and the idea of revolution, and most of them would have nothing.

The guerrillas look for their inspiration to the north. From Paris of 1968 there is the dream of students and workers uniting to defeat the enemies of 'the people'. The guerrillas have simplified the problems of Argentina. Like the campus and salon revolutionaries of the north, they have identified the enemy: the police. And so the social–intellectual diversions of the north are transformed, in the less intellectually stable south, into horrible reality. Dozens of policemen have been killed. And the police reply to terror with terror. They, too, kidnap and kill; they torture, concentrating on the genitals. A prisoner of the police jumps out of a window: *La Prensa* gives it a couple of inches. People are arrested and then, officially, 'released'; sometimes they reappear, sometimes they don't. A burned-out van is discovered in a street one morning. Inside there are two charred corpses: men who had been hustled out of their homes two days before. 'In what kind of country are we living?' one of the widows asks. But the next day she is calmer; she retracts the accusation against the police. Someone has 'visited' her.

'Friends of friends bring me these stories of atrocities,' Norman di Giovanni says, 'and it makes you sick. Yet no one here seems to be amazed by what's going on.' 'My wife's cousin was a *guerrillero*,' the provincial businessman says at lunch. 'He killed a policeman in Rosario. Then eight months ago, he disappeared. *Está muerto*. He's dead.' He has no more to say about it; and we talk of other matters.

On some evenings the jackbooted soldiers in black leather jackets patrol the pedestrian shopping street called Florida with their Alsatians: the dogs' tails close to their legs, their shoulders hunched, their ears thrown back. The police Chevrolets prowl the neon-lit streets unceasingly. There are policemen with machine guns everywhere. And there are the mounted police in slate grey; and the blue-helmeted anti-guerrilla motorcycle brigade; and those young men in well-cut suits who appear suddenly, plainclothesmen, jumping out of unmarked cars. Add the army's A M X tanks and Alouette helicopters. It is an impressive apparatus, and it works.

It is as if the energy of the state now goes into holding the state together. Law and order has become an end in itself: it is part of the Argentine sterility and waste. People are brave; they torture and are tortured; they die. But these are private events, scattered, muffled by a free but inadequate press that seems incapable of detecting a pattern in the events it reports. And perhaps the press is right. Perhaps very little of what happens in Argentina is really news, because there is no movement forward; nothing is being resolved. The nation appears to be playing a game with itself; and Argentine political life is like the life of an ant community or an African forest tribe: full of events, full of crisis and deaths, but life is only cyclical, and the year always ends as it begins. Even General Sánchez didn't, by his death, provoke a crisis. He tortured in vain, he died in vain. He simply lived for fifty-three years and, high as he was, has left no trace. Events are bigger than men. Only one man seems able to impose himself, to alter history now as he altered it in the past. And he waits at the Iron Gate.

Passion blinded our enemies [Perón wrote in 1956] and destroyed them ... The revolution [that overthrew me] is without a cause, because it is only a reaction ... The military people rule, but no one really obeys. Political chaos draws near. The economy, left to the management of clerks, gets worse day by day and ... anarchy threatens the social order ... These dictators who don't know too much and don't even know where they are going, who move from crisis to crisis, will end by losing their way on a road that leads nowhere.

The return of Perón, or the triumph of Peronism, is anticipated. It has been estimated that already between six and eight thousand million dollars have been shipped out of the country by Argentines. 'People are not involved,' the ambassador's wife says. 'And you must remember that anybody who has money is not an Argentine. Only people who don't have money are Argentines.'

But even at the level of wealth and security, even when escape plans have been drawn up, even, for instance, at this elegant dinner party in the Barrio Norte, passion breaks in. 'I'm *dying*,' the lady says abruptly, clenching her fists. 'I'm dying – I'm dying – I'm dying. It isn't a life any longer. Everybody clinging on by their fingertips. This place is *dead*. Sometimes I just go to bed after lunch and stay there.' The elderly butler wears white gloves; all the panelling in the room was imported from France at the turn of the century. (How easy and quick this Argentine aristocracy, how brief its settled life.) 'The streets are dug up, the lights are dim, the telephones don't answer.' The marijuana (forty-five dollars for the last half-kilo) passes; the mood does not alter. 'This used to be a great city and a great port. Twenty years ago. Now it's fucked up, baby.'

For intellectuals and artists as well, the better ones, who are not afraid of the outside world, there is this great anxiety of being imprisoned in Argentina and not being able to get out, of having one's creative years wasted by a revolution in which one can have no stake, or by a bloody-minded dictatorship, or just by chaos. Inflation and the crash of the peso have already trapped many. Menchi Sábat, the country's most brilliant cartoonist, says, 'It is easier for us to be on the moon by TV. But we don't know Bolivia or Chile or even Uruguay. The reason? Money. What we are seeing now is a kind of collective frenzy. Because before it was always easy here to get money. Now we are isolated. It isn't easy for people outside to understand what this means.'

The winter season still begins in May with the opera at the Colón Theatre; and orchestra seats at twenty-one dollars are quickly sold out. But the land has been despoiled of its most precious myth, the myth of wealth, wealth once so great, Argentines tell you, that you killed a cow and ate only the tongue, and the traveller on the pampa was free to kill and eat any cow, providing only that he left the skin for the landowner. Is it eight feet of topsoil that the humid pampa has? Or is it twelve? So rich, Argentina; such luck, with the land.

In 1850 there were fewer than a million Argentines; and Indian territory began one hundred miles west and south of Buenos Aires. Then, less than a hundred years ago, in a six-year carnage, the Indians were sought out and destroyed; and the pampa began to yield its treasure. Vast *estancias* on the stolen, bloody land: a sudden and jealous colonial aristocracy. Add immigrants, a labour force: in 1914 there were eight million Argentines. The immigrants, mainly from northern Spain and southern Italy, came not to be small holders or pioneers but to service the *estancias* and the port, Buenos Aires, that served the *estancias*. A vast and flourishing colonial economy, based on cattle and wheat, and attached to the British Empire; an urban proleteriat as sudden as the *estancia* aristocracy; a whole and sudden artificial society imposed on the flat, desolate land.

Borges, in his 1929 poem 'The Mythical Founding of Buenos Aires', remembers the proletarian spread of the city:

Una cigarrería sahumó como una rosa
el desierto. La tarde se había ahondado en ayeres,
los hombres compartieron un pasado ilusorio.
Sólo faltó una cosa: la vereda de enfrente.

Which in Alastair Reid's translation becomes:

A cigar store perfumed the desert like a rose.
The afternoon had established its yesterdays,
And men took on together an illusory past.
Only one thing was missing – the street had no
    other side.

A mí se me hace cuento que empezó Buenos Aires:
La juzgo tan eterna como el agua y el aire.

Hard to believe Buenos Aires had any beginning.
I feel it to be as eternal as air and water.

The half-made city is within Borges's memory. Now,
already, there is decay. The British Empire has withdrawn
ordenadamente, in good order; and the colonial agricultural
economy, attempting haphazardly to industrialize, to become balanced and autonomous, is in ruins. The
artificiality of the society shows. that absence of links
between men and men, between immigrant and immigrant, aristocrat and artisan, city dweller and *cabecita
negra*, the 'blackhead', the man from the interior; that
absence of a link between men and the meaningless flat
land. And the poor, who are Argentines, the sons and
grandsons of those recent immigrants, will now have to
stay.

They have always had their *curanderos* and *brujas*,
thaumaturges and witches; they know how to protect
themselves against the ghosts and poltergeists with which
they have peopled the alien land. But now a larger faith
is needed, some knowledge of a sheltering divinity. Without faith these abandoned Spaniards and Italians will
go mad.

At the end of May a Buenos Aires church advertised a special mass against the evil eye, *el mal de ojo*. 'If you've been damaged, or if you think you are being damaged, don't fail to come.' Five thousand city people turned up, many in motorcars. There were half a dozen stalls selling holy or beneficent objects; there were cubicles for religious–medical consultations, from thirty cents to a dollar a time. It was a little like a Saturday-morning market. The officiating priest said, 'Every individual is an individual source of power and is subject to imperceptible mental waves which can bring about ill-health or distress. This is the visible sign of the evil spirit.'

'I can never believe we are in 1972,' the publisher-bookseller says. 'It seems to me we are still in the year zero.' He isn't complaining; he himself trades in the occult and mystical, and his business is booming. Argentine middle-class mimicry of Europe and the United States, perhaps. But at a lower level the country is being swept by the new enthusiastic cult of *espiritismo*, a purely native affair of mediums and mass trances and miraculous cures, which claims the patronage of Jesus Christ and Mahatma Gandhi. The *espiritistas* don't talk of mental waves; their mediums heal by passing on intangible beneficent 'fluids'. The *espiritistas* say they have given up politics, and they revere Gandhi for his non-violence. They believe in reincarnation and the perfectibility of the spirit. They say that purgatory and hell exist now, on earth, and that man's only hope is to be born on a more evolved planet. Their goal is that life, in a 'definitive' disembodied world, where only superior spirits congregate.

Despair: a rejection of the land, a dream of nullity. But someone holds out hope; someone seeks to resanctify the land. With Perón at the Iron Gate is José López Rega, who has been his companion and private secretary through all the years of exile. Rega is known to have mystical leanings and to be interested in astrology and *espiritismo*; and he is said to be a man of great power now. An interview with him fills ten pages of a recent issue of *Las Bases*, the new Peronist fortnightly. Argentines are of many races, Rega says; but they all have native ancestors. The Argentine racial mixture has been 'enriched by Indian blood' and 'Mother Earth has purified it all ... I fight for liberty,' Rega goes on, 'because that's how I am made and because I feel stirring within me the blood of the Indian, whose land this is.' Now, for all its vagueness and unconscious irony, this is an astonishing statement, because, until this crisis, it was the Argentine's pride that his country was not 'niggered up' like Brazil or mestizo like Bolivia, but European; and it was his special anxiety that outsiders might think of Argentines as Indians. Now the Indian ghost is invoked, and a mystical, purifying claim is made on the blighted land.

Other people offer, as they have always offered, political and economic programmes. Perón and Peronism offer faith.

And they have a saint: Eva Perón. 'I remember I was very sad for many days,' she wrote in 1952 in *La Razón de Mi Vida (My Life's Cause)*, 'when I discovered that in the world there were poor people and rich people; and the strange thing is that the existence of the poor didn't cause me as much pain as the knowledge that at the same time there were people who were rich.' It was the basis of her political action. She preached a simple hate and a simple love. Hate for the rich: 'Shall we burn down the Barrio Norte?' she would say to the crowds. 'Shall I give you fire?' And love for 'the common people', *el pueblo*: she used that word again and again and made it part of the Peronist vocabulary. She levied tribute from everyone for her Eva Perón Foundation; and she sat until three or four or five in the morning in the Ministry of Labour, giving away foundation money to suppliants, dispensing a personal justice. This was her 'work': a child's vision of power, justice and revenge.

She died in 1952, when she was thirty-three. And now

in Argentina, after the proscribed years, the attempt to extirpate her name, she is a presence again. Her pictures are everywhere, touched up, seldom sharp, and often they seem deliberately garish, like religious pictures meant for the poor: a young woman of great beauty, with blonde hair, a very white skin and the very red lips of the 1940s.

She was of the people and of the land. She was born in 1919 in Los Toldos, the dreariest of pampa small towns, built on the site of an Indian encampment, 150 flat miles west of Buenos Aires. The town gives an impression of flatness, of total exposure below the high sky. The dusty brick houses, red or white, are low, flat-fronted and flat-roofed, with an occasional balustrade; the paraíso trees have whitewashed trunks and are severely pollarded; the wide streets, away from the centre, are still of dirt.

She was illegitimate; she was poor; and she lived for the first ten years of her life in a one-room house, which still stands. When she was fifteen she went to Buenos Aires to become an actress. Her speech was bad; she had a country girl's taste in clothes; her breasts were very small, her calves were heavy, and her ankles thickish. But within three months she had got her first job. And thereafter she charmed her way up. When she was twenty-five she met Perón; the following year they married.

Her commonness, her beauty, her success: they contribute to her sainthood. And her sexiness. '*Todos me acosan sexualmente,*' she once said with irritation, in her actress days. 'Everybody makes a pass at me.' She was the macho's ideal victim-woman – don't those red lips still speak to the Argentine macho of her reputed skill in fellatio? But very soon she was beyond sex, and pure again. At twenty-nine she was dying from cancer of the uterus, and haemorrhaging through the vagina; and her plumpish body began to waste away. Towards the end she weighed eighty pounds. One day she looked at some old official photographs of herself and began to cry. Another day she saw herself in a long mirror and said, 'When I think of the trouble I went to to keep my legs slim! *Ahora que me veo estas piernitas me asusto.* Now it frightens me to look at these matchsticks.'

But politically she never weakened. The Peronist revolution was going bad. Argentina's accumulated wartime wealth was running low; the colonial economy, unregenerated, plundered, mismanaged, was beginning to founder; the peso was falling; the workers, to whom so much had been given, were not always loyal. But she still cherished her especial pain that 'there were people who were rich'. Close to death, she told a gathering of provincial governors, 'We mustn't pay too much attention to people who talk to us of prudence. We must be fanatical.' The army was growing restive. She was willing to take them on. She wanted to arm the trade unions; and she did buy, through Prince Bernhard of the Netherlands, 5,000 automatic pistols and 1,500 machine guns, which, when they arrived, Perón, more prudent, gave to the police.

And all the time her private tragedy was being turned into the public passion play of the dictatorship. For her, who had turned Peronism into a religion, sainthood had long been decreed; and there is a story that for fifteen days before her death the man who was to embalm her was with her, to ensure that nothing was done that might damage the body. As soon as she died the embalming contract was signed. Was it for $100,000 or $300,000? The reports are confused. Dr Ara, the Spanish embalmer – 'a master', Perón called him – had first to make the body ready for a fifteen-day lying in state. The actual embalming took six months. The process remains secret. Dr Ara, according to a Buenos Aires newspaper, has devoted two chapters of his memoirs (which are to be published only after his death) to the emblaming of Eva Perón; colour pictures of the corpse are also promised. Reports suggest that the blood was first replaced by alcohol, and then by heated glycerin (Perón himself says 'paraffin and other special matter'), which was pumped in through the heel and an ear.

'I went three times to look at Evita,' Perón wrote in 1956, after his overthrow, and when the embalmed body had disappeared. 'The doors ... were like the gates of eternity.' He had the impression that she was only sleeping. The first time he went he wanted to touch her, but he feared that at the touch of his warm hand the body would turn to dust. Ara said, 'Don't worry. She's as whole [*intacta*] now as when she was alive.'

And now, twenty years later, her embalmed wasted body, once lost, now found, and no bigger, they say, than that of a twelve-year-old girl, only the blonde hair as rich as in the time of health, waits with Perón at the Iron Gate.

It came as a surprise, this *villa miseria* or shantytown just beside the brown river in the Palermo district, not far from the great park, Buenos Aires's equivalent of the Bois de Boulogne, where people go riding. A shantytown, with unpaved streets and black runnels of filth, but the buildings were of brick, with sometimes an upper storey: a settled place, more than fifteen years old, with shops and signs. Seventy thousand people lived there, nearly all Indians, blank and slightly imbecilic in appearance, from the north and from Bolivia and Paraguay; so that suddenly you were reminded that you were not in Paris or Europe but in South America. The priest in charge was one of the 'Priests for the Third World'. He wore a black leather jacket and his little concrete shed of a church, over-simple, rocked with some amplified Argentine song. It had been whispered to me that the priest came of a very good family; and perhaps the change of company had made him vain. He was of course a Peronist, and he said that all his Indians were Peronist. 'Only an

Argentine can understand Peronism. I can talk to you for five years about Peronism, but you will never understand.'

But couldn't we try? He said Peronism wasn't concerned with economic growth; they rejected the consumer society. But hadn't he just been complaining about the unemployment in the interior, the result of government folly, that was sending two Indians into his shantytown for every one that left? He said he wasn't going to waste his time talking to a *norteamericano*; some people were concerned only with G N P. And, leaving us, he bore down, all smiles, on some approaching Indians. The river wind was damp, the concrete shed unheated, and I wanted to leave. But the man with me was uneasy. He said we should at least wait and tell the father I wasn't an American. We did so. And the father, abashed, explained that Peronism was really concerned with the development of the human spirit. Such a development had taken place in Cuba and China; in those countries they had turned their backs on the industrial society.*

These lawyers had been represented to me as a group working for 'civil rights'. They were young, stylishly dressed, and they were meeting that morning to draft a petition against torture. The top-floor flat was scruffy and bare; visitors were scrutinized through the peephole; everybody whispered; and there was a lot of cigarette smoke. Intrigue, danger. But one of the lawyers was diverted by my invitation to lunch, and at lunch – he was a hearty and expensive eater – he made it clear that the torture they were protesting against wasn't to be confused with the torture in Perón's time.

He said, 'When justice is the justice of the people, men sometimes commit excesses. But in the final analysis, the important thing is that justice should be done in

* The priest was killed two years later, in 1974, by unknown gunmen, and for a few days had poster fame as a Peronist martyr.

the name of the people.' Who were the enemies of the people? His response was tabulated and swift. 'American imperialism. And its native allies. The oligarchy, the dependent bourgeoisie, Zionism, and the "sepoy" left. By sepoys we mean the Communist Party and socialism in general.' It seemed a comprehensive list. Who were the Peronists? 'Peronism is a revolutionary national movement. There is a great difference between a movement and a party. We are not Stalinists, and a Peronist is anyone who calls himself a Peronist and acts like a Peronist.'

The lawyer, for all his anti-Jewish feeling, was a Jew; and he came of an anti-Peronist middle-class family. In 1970 he had met Perón in Madrid, and he had been dazzled; his voice shook when he quoted Perón's words. He had said to Perón, 'General, why don't you declare war on the regime and then put yourself at the head of all the true Peronists?' Perón replied, 'I am the conductor of a national movement. I have to conduct the whole movement, in its totality.'

'There are no internal enemies,' the trade union leader said, with a smile. But at the same time he thought that torture would continue in Argentina. 'A world without torture is an ideal world.' And there was torture and torture. '*Depende de quién sea torturado*. It depends on who is tortured. An evildoer, that's all right. But a man who's trying to save the country – that's something else. Torture isn't only the electric prod, you know. Poverty is torture, frustration is torture.' He was urbane; I had been told he was the most intellectual of the Peronist trade union leaders. He had been punctual; his office was uncluttered and neat; on his desk, below glass, there was a large photograph of the young Perón.

The first Peronist revolution was based on the myth of wealth, of a land waiting to be plundered. Now the wealth has gone. And Peronism is like part of the poverty.

It is protest, despair, faith, machismo, magic, *espiritismo*, revenge. It is everything and nothing. Remove Perón, and hysteria will be uncontrollable. Remove the armed forces, sterile guardians of law and order, and Peronism, triumphant, will disintegrate into a hundred scattered fights, every man identifying his own enemy.

'Violence, in the hands of the people, isn't violence: it is justice.' This statement of Perón's was printed on the front page of a recent issue of *Fe*, a Peronist paper. So, in sinister mimicry, the south twists the revolutionary jargon of the north. Where jargon turns living issues into abstractions ('Torture will disappear in Argentina,' the Trotskyist said, 'only with a workers' government and the downfall of the bourgeoisie'), and where jargon ends by competing with jargon, people don't have causes. They only have enemies; only the enemies are real. It has been the South American nightmare since the break-up of the Spanish Empire.

Was Eva Perón blonde or brunette? Was she born in 1919 or 1922? Was she born in the little town of Los Toldos, or in Junín, forty kilometres away? Well, she was a brunette who dyed her hair blonde; she was born in 1919 but said 1922 (and had her birth record destroyed in 1945); she spent the first ten years of her life in Los Toldos but ever afterwards disclaimed the town. No one will know why. Don't go to her autobiography, *La Razón de Mi Vida*, which used to be prescribed reading in Argentine schools. That doesn't contain a fact or a date; and it was written by a Spaniard, who later complained that the book he wrote had been much altered by the Peronist authorities.

So the truth begins to disappear; it is not relevant to the legend. Masses are held in Eva Perón's memory, and students now turn up in numbers; but her life is not the subject of inquiry. Unmarked, seldom visited (though a woman remembers that once some television people came), the one-room house in brown brick in Los Toldos crumbles. The elderly garage owner next door (two vehicles in his garage, one an engineless Model T), to whom the house now belongs, uses it as a storeroom. Grass sprouts from the flat roof, and the corrugated-iron roof collapses over the patio at the back.

Only one biography of Eva Perón has been attempted in Argentina. It was to be in two volumes, but the publisher went bankrupt and the second volume hasn't appeared. Had she lived, Eva Perón would now be only fifty-three. There are hundreds of people alive who knew her. But in two months I found it hard to get beyond what was well known. Memories have been edited; people deal in panegyric or hate, and the people who hate refuse to talk about her. The anguish of those early years at Los Toldos has been successfully suppressed. The Eva Perón story has been lost; there is now only the legend.

One evening, after his classes at the Catholic University, and while the police sirens screamed outside, Borges told me: 'We had a sense that the whole thing should have been forgotten. Had the newspapers been silent, there would have been no Peronism today – the Peronistas were at first ashamed of themselves. If I were facing a public audience I would never use his name. I would say *el prófugo*, the fugitive, *el dictador*. The way in poetry one avoids certain words – if I used his name in a poem the whole thing would fall to pieces.'

It is the Argentine attitude: suppress, ignore. Many of the records of the Peronist era have been destroyed. If today the middle-class young are Peronists, and students sing the old song of the dictatorship –

> *Perón, Perón, qué grande sos!*
> *Mi general, cuánto valés!*

> Perón, Perón, how great you are!
> How good and strong, my general!

– if the dictatorship, even in its excesses, is respectable again, it isn't because the past has been investigated and the record modified. It is only that many people have revised their attitudes towards the established legend. They have changed their minds.

There is no history in Argentina. There are no archives; there are only graffiti and polemics and school lessons. Schoolchildren in white dustcoats are regularly taken round the Cabildo building in the Plaza de Mayo in Buenos Aires to see the relics of the War of Independence. The event is glorious; it stands in isolation; it is not related, in the text books or in the popular mind, to what immediately followed: the loss of law, the seeking out of the enemy, endless civil wars, gangster rule.

Borges said on another evening: 'The history of Argentina is the history of its separateness from Spain.' How did Perón fit into that? 'Perón represented the scum of the earth.' But he surely also stood for something that was Argentine? Unfortunately, I have to admit that he's an Argentine – an Argentine of today.' Borges is a *criollo*, someone whose ancestors came to Argentina before the great immigrant rush, before the country became what it is; and for the contemplation of his country's history Borges substitutes ancestor worship. Like many Argentines, he has an idea of Argentina; anything that doesn't fit into this is to be rejected. And Borges is Argentina's greatest man.

An attitude to history, an attitude to the land. Magic is important in Argentina; the country is full of witches and magicians and thaumaturges and mediums. But the visitor must ignore this side of Argentine life because, he is told, it isn't real. The country is full of *estancias*; but the visitor mustn't go to that particular *estancia* because it isn't typical. But it exists, it works. Yes, but it isn't real. Nor is that real, nor that, nor that. So the whole country is talked away; and the visitor finds himself directed to the equivalent of a guacho curio shop. It isn't the Argentina that anyone inhabits, least of all one's guides; but *that* is real, *that* is Argentina. 'Basically we all love the country,' an Anglo-Argentine said. 'But we would like it to be in our own image. And many of us are now suffering for our fantasies.' A collective refusal to see, to come to terms with the land: an artificial, fragmented colonial society, made deficient and bogus by its myths.

To be Argentine was not to be South American. It was to be European; and many Argentines became European, of Europe. The land that was the source of their wealth became no more than their base. For these Argentine–Europeans, Buenos Aires and Mar del Plata became resort towns, with a seasonal life. Between the wars there was a stable Argentine community of 100,000 in Paris; the peso was the peso then.

'Many people think,' Borges said, 'that quite the best thing that could have happened here would have been an English victory [in 1806–7, when the British twice raided Buenos Aires]. At the same time I wonder whether being a colony does any good – so provincial and dull.'

But to be European in Argentina was to be colonial in the most damaging way. It was to be parasitic. It was to claim – as the white communities of the Caribbean colonies claimed – the achievements and authority of Europe as one's own. It was to ask less of oneself (in Trinidad, when I was a child, it was thought that the white and the rich needed no education). It was to accept, out of a false security, a second-rateness for one's own society.

And there was the wealth of Argentina: the British railways taking the wheat and the meat from all the corners of the pampa to the port of Buenos Aires, for shipment to England. There was no pioneer or nation-making myth of hard work and reward. The land was empty and very flat and very rich; it was inexhaustible;

and it was infinitely forgiving. *Dios arregla de noche la macana que los Argentinos hacen de día*: God puts right at night the mess the Argentines make by day.

To be Argentine was to inhabit a magical, debilitating world. Wealth and Europeanness concealed the colonial realities of an agricultural society which had needed little talent and had produced little, which had needed no great men and had produced none. 'Nothing *happened* here,' Norman di Giovanni said with irritation one day. And everyone, from Borges down, says, 'Buenos Aires is a small town.' Eight million people: a monstrous plebeian sprawl, mean, repetitive and meaningless: but only a small town, eaten up by colonial doubt and malice. When the real world is felt to be outside, everyone at home is inadequate and fraudulent. A waiter in Mendoza said, 'Argentines don't work. We can't do anything big. Everything we do is small and petty.' An artist said, 'There are very few *professionals* here. By that I mean people who know what to do with themselves. No one knows why he is doing any particular job. For that reason, if you are doing what I do, then you are my enemy.'

Camelero, chanta: these are everyday Argentine words. A *camelero* is a line-shooter, a man who really has nothing to sell. The man who promised to take me to an *estancia*, and in his private airplane, was only doing *camelo*. The *chanta* is the man who will sell everything, the man without principles, the hollow man. Almost everybody, from the president down, is dismissed by somebody as a *chanta*.

The other word that recurs is *mediocre*. Argentines detest the mediocre and fear to be thought mediocre. It was one of Eva Perón's words of abuse. For her the Argentine aristocracy was always mediocre. And she was right. In a few years she shattered the myth of Argentina as an aristocratic colonial land. And no other myth, no other idea of the land, has been found to take its place.

2   Borges and the Bogus Past

Borges, speaking of the fame of writers, said: 'The important thing is the image you create of yourself in other people's minds. Many people think of Burns as a mediocre poet. But he stands for many things, and people like him. That image – as with Byron – may in the end be more important than the work.'

Borges is a great writer, a sweet and melancholy poet; and people who know Spanish well revere him as a writer of a direct, unrhetorical prose. But his Anglo-American reputation as a blind and elderly Argentine, the writer of a very few, very short, and very mysterious stories, is so inflated and bogus that it obscures his greatness. It has possibly cost him the Nobel Prize; and it may well happen that when the bogus reputation declines, as it must, the good work may also disappear.

The irony is that Borges, at his best, is neither mysterious nor difficult. His poetry is accessible; much of it is even romantic. His themes have remained constant for the last fifty years: his military ancestors, their deaths in battle, death itself, time, and old Buenos Aires. And there are about a dozen successful stories. Two or three are straightforward, even old-fashioned, detective stories (one was published in *Ellery Queen's Mystery Magazine*). Some deal, quite cinematically, with Buenos Aires low life at the turn of the century. Gangsters are given epic stature; they rise, they are challenged, and sometimes they run away.

The other stories – the ones that have driven the critics crazy – are in the nature of intellectual jokes. Borges takes a word like 'immortal' and plays with it. Suppose, he says, men were really immortal. Not just men who had grown old and wouldn't die, but indestructible vigorous men, surviving for eternity. What would be the result? His answer – which is his story – is that every conceivable experience would at some time befall every man, that every man would at some time assume every conceivable character, and that Homer (the disguised hero of this particular story) might in the eigheenth century even forget he had written the *Odyssey*. Or take the word 'unforgettable'. Suppose something were truly unforgettable, and couldn't be forgotten for a single second; suppose this thing came, like a coin, into your possession. Exetend that idea. Suppose there were a man – but no, he has to be a boy – who could forget nothing, whose memory therefore ballooned and ballooned with all the unforgettable details of every minute of his life.

These are some of Borges's intellectual games. And perhaps his most successful piece of prose writing, which is also his shortest, is a pure joke. It is called 'Of Exactitude in Science' and is meant to be an extract from a seventeenth-century book of travel:

> In that Empire, the craft of Cartography attained such Perfection that the Map of a Single province covered the space of an entire City, and the Map of the Empire itself an entire Province. In the course of Time, these Extensive maps were found somehow wanting, and so the College of Cartographers evolved a Map of the Empire that was of the same Scale as the Empire and coincided with it point for point. Less attentive to the Study of Cartography, succeeding Generations came to judge a map of such Magnitude cumbersome and, not without Irreverence, abandoned it to the Rigours of sun and Rain. In the western Deserts, tattered Fragments of the Map are still to be found, Sheltering an occasional Beast or beggar; in the whole Nation no other relic is left of the Discipline of Geography.

This is absurd and perfect: the accurate parody, the grotesque idea. Borges's puzzle and jokes can be addictive. But they have to be recognized for what they are; they cannot always support the metaphysical interpretations they receive. There is, though, much to attract the academic critic. Some of Borges's hoaxes require – and sometimes disappear below – an extravagant display of curious learning. And there is the occasional baroque language of the early stories.

'The Circular Ruins' – an elaborate, almost science fiction story about a dreamer discovering that he himself exists only in somebody else's dream – begins: '*Nadie lo vió desembarcar en la unánime noche.*' Literally, 'Nobody saw him disembark in the unanimous night.' Norman Thomas di Giovanni, who has been translating Borges full-time for the last four years, and has done more than anyone else to push Borges's work in the English-speaking world, says:

> You can imagine how much has been written about that 'unanimous'. I went to Borges with two translations, 'surrounding' and 'encompassing'. And I said, 'Borges, what did you really mean by the unanimous night? That doesn't mean anything. If the unanimous night, why not the tea-drinking night, or the card-playing night?' And I was astonished by his answer. He said, 'Di Giovanni, that's just one example of the irresponsible way I used to write.' We used 'encompassing' in the translation. But a lot of the professors didn't like losing their unanimous night ...

There was this woman. She wrote an essay on Borges for a book. She didn't know any Spanish and was basing her essay on two rather mediocre English translations. A long essay, about forty pages. And one of the *crucial* points was that Borges wrote a very Latinate prose. I had to point out to her that Borges could not help but write a Latinate prose, because he wrote in Spanish, and Spanish is a dialect of Latin. She didn't consult anybody when she was laying the foundation. At the end she calls out 'Help!' and you run up and see this enormous skyscraper sinking in quicksand.

Di Giovanni went with Borges on a lecture tour of the United States in 1969:

> Borges is a gentleman. When people come up and tell him what his stories really mean – after all, he only wrote them – he has the most wonderful line you've ever heard. 'Ah, thank you! You've enriched my story. You've made me a great gift. I've come all the way from Buenos Aires to X – say Lubbock, Texas – to find out this truth about myself and my story.'

Borges has for years enjoyed a considerable reputation in the Spanish-speaking world. But in 'An Autobiographical Essay', which was published as a 'Profile' in the *New Yorker* in 1970, he says that until he won the Formentor Prize in 1961 – he was sixty-two then – he was 'practically invisible – not only abroad but at home in Buenos Aires'. This is the kind of exaggeration that dismays some of his early Argentine supporters; and there are those who would say that his 'irresponsibility' has grown with his fame. But Borges has always been irresponsible. Buenos Aires is a small town; and what perhaps was inoffensive when Borges belonged only to this small town becomes less so when foreigners queue up for interviews. Once, no doubt, Borges's celebration of his military ancestors and their deaths in battle flattered the whole society, giving it a sense of the past and of completeness. Now it appears to exclude, to proclaim a private grandeur; and to many it is only egotistical and presumptuous. It is not easy to be famous in a small town.

Borges gives many interviews. And every interview seems to be like every other interview. He seems to make questions irrelevant; he plays, as one Argentine lady said, his *discos*, his records; he performs. He says that the Spanish language is his 'doom'. He criticizes Spain and the Spaniards: he still fights that colonial war, in which, however, the old issues have become confused with a simpler Argentine prejudice against the poor and backward immigrants from northern Spain. He makes his tasteless, and expected, jokes about the pampa Indians. Tasteless because just twenty years before he was born these Indians were systematically exterminated; and yet expected, because slaughter on this scale becomes acceptable only if the victims are made ridiculous. He talks about Chesterton, Stevenson and Kipling. He talks about Old English with all the enthusiasm of a man who has picked up an academic subject by himself. He talks about his English ancestors.

It is a curiously colonial performance. His Argentine past is part of his distinction; he offers it as such; and he is after all a patriot. He honours the flag, an example of which flies from the balcony of his office in the National Library (he is the director). And he is moved by the country's anthem. But at the same time he seems anxious to proclaim his separateness from Argentina. The performance might seem aimed at Borges's new Anglo-American campus audience, whom in so many ways it flatters. But the attitudes are old.

In Buenos Aires it is still remembered that in 1955, just a few days after Perón was overthrown and that nine-year dictatorship was over, Borges gave a lecture on – of all subjects – Coleridge to the ladies of the Association for English Culture. Some of Coleridge's lines, Borges said, were among the best in English poetry, '*es decir la poesía*': 'that is to say poetry'. And those four words, at a time of national rejoicing, were like a gratuitous assault on the Argentine soul.

Norman di Giovanni tells a balancing story.

In December 1969, we were at Georgetown University in Washington, D.C. The man doing the introduction was an Argentine from Tucumán and he took advantage of the occasion to point out to the audience that the military repression had closed the university in Tucumán. Borges was totally oblivious of what the man had said until we were on our way to the airport. Then someone began to talk about it and Borges was suddenly very angry. 'Did you hear what that man said? That they'd closed the university in Tucumán.' I questioned him about his rage, and he said, 'That man was attacking my country. They can't talk that way about my country.' I said, 'Borges, what do you mean, "that man"? That man is an Argentine. And he comes from Tucumán. And what he says is true. The military *have* closed the university.'

Borges is of medium height. His nearly sightless eyes and his stick add to the distinction of his appearance. He dresses carefully. He says he is a middle-class writer; and a middle-class writer shouldn't be either a dandy or too affectedly casual. He is courtly: he thinks, with Sir Thomas Browne, that a gentleman is someone who tries to give the least amount of trouble. 'But you should look that up in *Religio Medici*.' It might seem then that in his accessibility, his willingness to give lengthy interviews which repeat the other interviews he has given, Borges combines the middle-class ideal of self-effacement and the gentleman's manners with the writer's privacy, the writer's need to save himself for his work.

There are hints of this privacy (in accessibilty) in the way he likes to be addressed. Perhaps no more than half a dozen people have the privilege of calling him by his first name, Jorge, which they turn into 'Georgie'. To everyone else he likes to be just 'Borges' without the *Señor*, which he considers Spanish and pompous. 'Borges' is, of course, distancing.

And even the fifty-page 'Autobiographical Essay' doesn't violate his privacy. It is like another interview. It says little that is new. His birth in Buenos Aires in

1899, the son of a lawyer; his military ancestors; the family's seven-year sojourn in Europe from 1914 to 1921 (when the peso was valuable, and Europe was cheaper than Buenos Aires): all this is told again in outline, as in an interview. And the essay quickly becomes no more than a writer's account of his writing life, of the books he read and the books he wrote, the literary groups he joined and the magazines he founded. The life is missing. There is the barest sketch of the crisis he must have gone through in his late thirties and early forties, when – the family money lost – he was doing all kinds of journalism; when his father died, and he himself fell seriously ill and 'feared for [his] mental integrity'; when he worked as an assistant in a municipal library, well known as a writer outside the library, unknown inside it. 'I remember a fellow employee's once noting in an encyclopaedia the name of a certain Jorge Luis Borges – a fact that set him wondering at the coincidence of our identical names and birth dates.'

'Nine years of solid unhappiness,' he says; but he gives the period only four pages. The privacy of Borges begins to appear a forbidding thing.

> *Un dios me ha concedido*
> *Lo que es dado saber a los mortales.*
> *Por todo el continente anda mi nombre;*
> *No he vivido. Quisiera ser otro hombre.*

Mark Strand translates:

> I have been allowed
> That which is given mortal man to know.
> The whole continent knows my name.
> I have not lived. I want to be someone else.

This is Borges on Emerson; but it might be Borges on Borges. Life, in the 'Autobiographical Essay', is indeed missing. So that all that is important in the man has to be found in the work, which with Borges is essentially the poetry. And all the themes he has explored over a long life are contained, as he himself says, in his very first book of poems, published in 1923, a book printed in five days, three hundred copies, given away free.

Here is the military ancestor dying in battle. Here, already, at the age of twenty-four, the contemplation of glory turns into the meditation on death and time and the 'glass jewels' of the individual life:

> ... *cuando tú mismo eres la continuación realizada*
> *de quienes no alcanzaron tu tiempo*
> *y otros serán (y son) tu inmortalidad en la tierra.*

In W. S. Merwin's translation:

> ... when you yourself are the embodied continuance
> of those who did not live into your time
> and others will be (and are) your immortality on earth.

Somewhere around that time life stopped; and all that has been followed has been literature: a concern with words, an unending attempt to stay with, and not to betray, the emotions of that so particular past.

> I am myself and I am him today,
> The man who died, the man whose blood and name
> Are mine.

This is Norman di Giovanni's translation of a poem written forty-three years after that first book:

> *Soy, pero soy también el otro, el muerto,*
> *El otro de mi sangre y de mi nombre.*

Since the writing of that first book nothing, except perhaps his discovery of Old English poetry, has provided Borges with matter for such intense meditation. Not even the bitter Perón years, when he was ' "promoted" out of the library to the inspectorship of poultry and rabbits in the public markets', and resigned. Nor his brief, unhappy marriage late in life, once the subject of magazine articles, and still a subject of gossip in Buenos Aires. Nor his continuing companionship with his mother, now aged ninety-six.

'In 1910, the centenary of the Argentine Republic, we thought of Argentina as an honourable country and we had no doubt that the nations would come flocking in. Now the country is in a bad way. We are being threatened by the return of the horrible man.' This is how Borges speaks of Perón: he prefers not to use the name.

I get any number of personal threats. Even my mother. They rang her up in the small hours – two or three in the morning – and somebody said to her in a very gruff kind of voice, the voice you associate with a *Peronista*, 'I've got to kill you and your son.' My mother said, 'Why?' 'Because I am a *Peronista*.' My mother said, 'As far as my son is concerned, he is over seventy and practically blind. But in my case I should advise you to waste no time because I am ninety-five and may die on your hands before you can kill me.' Next morning I told my mother I thought I had heard the telephone ringing in the night. 'Did I dream that?' She said, 'Just some fool.' She's not only witty. But courageous ... I don't see what I can do about it – the political situation. But I think I should do what I can, having military men in my family.

Borges's first book of poems was called *Fervour of Buenos Aires*. In it, he said in his preface, he was attempting to celebrate the new and expanding city in a special way. 'Akin to the Romans, who would murmur the words *"numen inest"* on passing through a wood, "Here dwells a god," my verses declare, stating the wonder of the streets ... Everyday places become, little by little, holy.'

But Borges has not hallowed Buenos Aires. The city the visitor sees is not the city of the poems, the way Simla (as new and artificial as Buenos Aires) remains, after all these years, the city of Kipling's stories. Kipling looked hard at a real town. Borges's Buenos Aires is private, a city of the imagination. And now the city itself is in decay. In Borges's own Southside some old buildings survive, with their mighty front doors and their receding patios, each patio differently tiled. But more often the inner patios have been blocked up; and many of the old buildings have been pulled down. Elegance, if in this plebeian immigrant city elegance really ever existed outside the vision of expatriate architects, has vanished; there is now only disorder.

The white and pale blue Argentine flag that hangs out into Mexico Street from the balcony of Borges's office in the National Library is dingy with dirt and fumes. And consider this building, perhaps the finest in the area, which was used as a hospital and a gaol in the time of the gangster-dictator Rosas more than 120 years ago. There is beauty still in the spiked wall, the tall iron gates, the huge wooden doors. But inside, the walls peel; the windows in the central patio are broken; farther in, courtyard opening into courtyard, washing hangs in a corridor, steps are broken, and a metal spiral staircase is blocked with junk. This is a government office, a department of the Ministry of Labour: it speaks of an administration that has seized up, a city that is dying, a country that hasn't really worked.

Walls everywhere are scrawled with violent slogans; guerrillas operate in the streets; the peso falls; the city is full of hate. The bloody-minded slogan repeats: *Rosas vuelve*, Rosas is coming back. The country awaits a new terror.

Numen inest, here dwells a god: the poet's incantation hasn't worked. The military ancestors died in battle, but those petty battles and wasteful deaths have led to nothing. Only in Borges's poetry do those heroes inhabit 'an epic universe, sitting tall in the saddle': '*alto ... en su épico universo*'. And this is his great creation: Argentina as a simple mythical land, a complete epic world, of 'republics, cavalry and mornings': *'las repúblicas, los caballos y las mañanas'*, of battles fought, the fatherland established, the great city created and the 'streets with names recurring from the past in my blood'.

That is the vision of art. And yet, out of this mythical Argentina of his creation, Borges reaches out, through his English grandmother, to his English ancestors and, through them, to their language 'at its dawn'. 'People tell me I look English now. When I was younger I didn't look English. I was darker. I didn't feel English. Not at all. Maybe feeling English came to me through reading.' And though Borges doesn't acknowledge it, a recurring theme in the later stories is of Nordics growing degenerate in a desolate Argentine landscape. Scottish Guthries become mestizo Gutres and no longer even know the Bible; an English girl becomes an Indian savage; men called Nilsen forget their origins and live like animals with the bestial sex code of the macho whoremonger.

Borges said at our first meeting, 'I don't write about degenerates.' But another time he said, 'The country was enriched by men thinking essentially of Europe and the United States. Only the civilized people. The gauchos were very simple-minded. Barbarians.' When we talked of Argentine history he said, 'There is a pattern. Not an obvious pattern. I myself can't see the wood for the trees.' And later he added, 'Those civil wars are now meaningless.'

Perhaps, then, parallel with the vision of art, there has developed, in Borges, a subsidiary vision, however unacknowledged, of reality. And now, at any rate, the real world can no longer be denied.

In the middle of May Borges went for a few days to Montevideo in Uruguay. Montevideo was one of the cities of his childhood, a city of 'long, lazy holidays'. But now Uruguay, the most educated country in South America, was, in the words of an Argentine, 'a caricature of a country', bankrupt, like Argentina, after wartime wealth, and tearing itself to pieces. Montevideo was a city at war; guerrillas and soldiers fought in the streets. One day, while Borges was there, four soldiers were shot and killed.

I saw Borges when he came back. A pretty girl helped him down the steps at the Catholic University. He looked more frail; his hands shook more easily. He had shed his sprightly interview manner. He was full of the disaster of Montevideo; he was distressed. Montevideo was something else he had lost. In one poem 'mornings in Montevideo' are among the things for which he thanks 'the divine labyrinth of causes and effects'. Now Montevideo, like Buenos Aires, like Argentina, was gracious only in his memory, and in his art.

3   Kamikaze in Montevideo

October–November 1973

Interest rates went down in Uruguay this year. Last year, at the height of the Tupamaro crisis, you could borrow money at 60 per cent. The interest, payable in advance, was immediately deducted from the loan; so that, having borrowed a million pesos, you left the bank with 400,000. And that was good business, with the peso losing half its value against the dollar during the year, and with inflation running at 92 per cent.

Now it is a little less frenzied. The Tupamaros – there were about five thousand of them, mainly townspeople from impoverished middle-class families – have been destroyed. The army – essentially rural, lower middle-class – is in control and rules by decree. Interest rates have dropped to around 42 per cent, with the taxes; and inflation this year has been kept down to 60 per cent. 'Prices here don't just rise every day,' the businessman said. 'They also rise every night.'

Yet until the other day, they tell you in Uruguay, road-workers could be seen grilling their lunchtime steaks in the open air; and the Uruguay peso was known as the *peso oro*, the gold peso. In 1953 there were 3 pesos to the U.S. dollar; today there are 900.

'My father bought a house in 1953 with a 6 per cent loan from the Mortgage Bank. At the end, in 1968, he was still paying thirty pesos a month on his mortgage.' Thirty pesos: twelve cents, ten pence. 'That may be funny to you. For us it is a tragedy. Our Parliament refused to revalue mortgage repayments – the politicians didn't want to lose votes. So everybody had his house as a gift. But they condemned the future generations.'

The law has now been changed. Interest rates, like salaries, are tied to the cost-of-living index; and the Mortgage Bank these days offers depositors 56 per cent – 7 per cent true interest, 49 per cent the inflationary 'adjustment'.

Mr Palatnik, the advertising man who handles the Mortgage Bank campaign, has also been engaged by the military government to help calm the country down. And, to the disgust and alarm of Left and extreme Right, Mr Palatnik doesn't appear to be failing. He hasn't so far made himself or the government absurd. Again and again on television, in the commercial breaks in the Argentine soap operas, after the talk of government plans, hope comes in the form of a challenge: *'Tenga confianza en el país, y póngale el hombro al Uruguay.'* Literally: 'Have faith in the country, and put your shoulder to Uruguay.'

But in Uruguay these days it is hard not to offend. *New Dawn*, the weekly newspaper of a new right-wing youth group ('Family, Tradition, Property'), published a strong attack on Mr Palatnik, with a distinctly anti-Semitic cartoon. Mr Palatnik, who is middle-aged, challenged the editor to a duel. He sent his *padrinos* to the

New Dawn office, but the challenge wasn't accepted. The *New Dawn* group isn't important; but, like many businessmen in Montevideo, Mr Palatnik now carries a gun.

The precaution is excessive. The army at the moment is in control and on the offensive; it continues to arrest and interrogate; the days of guerrilla kidnap in Montevideo are over. Montevideo, so dangerous last year, is now safer than Buenos Aires; and some of the more ransomable American business executives in Argentina have moved across the Río de la Plata to Montevideo, to the red-brick tower of the Victoria Plaza Hotel in the main square, with the equestrian statue of Artigas, the founder of the Uruguayan state, in the centre.

Government House is on the side of the square. There are sentries in nineteenth-century uniform, but also real soldiers with real guns. On another side of the square the Palace of Justice, begun six years ago, stands unfinished in the immense crater of its foundations. Grass, level and lush as if sown, grows from the concrete beams, and the concrete columns are stained with rust from the reinforcing steel rods.

Montevideo is safe. But the money has run out in a country whose official buildings, in the days of wealth, were of marble, granite and bronze. All the extravagant woodwork in the Legislative Palace, all the marquetry that rises from floor to ceiling in the library, was made in Italy and shipped out, they say, in mahogany crates. And that was just fifty years ago. Now the palace is without a function, and soldiers, making small gestures with their guns, urge passers-by to keep their distance.

Fifty years ago, before people built on the sea, the fashionable area was the Prado: great houses, some gothic follies, great gardens. The Prado park is now tended only in parts; the once-famous rose garden runs wild. Beyond the bridge with the tarnished *Belle Époque* sphinxes, a long drive, shaded by eucalyptus, plane and fir, leads to the Prado Hotel, still apparently whole, with its green walks and balustraded terraces and a fountain that still plays. But the asphalt forecourt is cracked; the lamp standards and urns are empty; the great yellow building – *Jules Knab arq 1911* incised halfway up – has been abandoned.

Montevideo is in parts a ghost city, its *nouveau riche* splendour still new. It is a city full of statues – copies of the *David*, the Colleoni statue in Venice, elaborate historical tableaux in bronze. But letters have dropped off inscriptions and have not been replaced; and the public clocks on street corners have everywhere stopped. The plane trees in the centre are not old; tall carved doors still open on to marble halls with fine ceilings that still look new. But the shops have little to offer; the pavements are broken; the streets are too full of people selling chocolate and sweets and other little things. The three or four fair restaurants that survive – in a city of more than a million – do not always have meat; and the bread is made partly of sorghum.

Even without the slogans on the walls – STOP TORTURING SASSANO, THE MILITARY ARE TORTURING SERENY, DEATH TO THE DICTATORSHIP, TUPAMAROS RENEGADES THIEVES SWINE, PUTAMAROS [*puta*, a whore] – the visitor would know that he is in a city where, as in a fairy story, a hidden calamity has occurred. A fabulous city, created all at once, and struck down almost as soon as it had been created.

'The country has grown sad,' the artist said. He survives by living to himself, doing his work, and pretending that Uruguay is somewhere else. He doesn't listen to the radio or watch television or read the newspapers. What – apart from the football – had he missed in that morning's *El Pais*? A plane hijacked to Bolivia; five hundred secondary-school students suspended; five 'extremists', three of them university students, indicted by the military court for 'conspiring against the Constitution'.

When Uruguay was rich, politics were a matter of personalities and the army hardly existed. Now the money has run out, and the little country – almost as big as Britain, but with less than three million people – tears itself apart.

'The army came for me at four in the morning. In the gaol – they play pop music in the torture cells – I was made to stand with my feet together for ten hours. Then I was given the "submarine". I was winded by a heavy blow in the stomach and my head was held under water. They're expert now. But they've had accidents. Then I was made to stand again. When I collapsed I was prodded between the legs with a bayonet.' The 'submarine' is 'soft' torture. People who have been burned by the electric prod don't talk about their experiences.

Everyone in Uruguay, whether on the Right or Left, knows now – sixty years too late – where the trouble started. It started with the president called Batlle (pronounced *Bajhay*); it started with the welfare state Batlle, after a visit to Switzerland, began to impose on Uruguay just before the First World War.

Uruguay had the money. Her exports of meat and wool made her rich; the peso was on a par with the dollar. 'In those days,' the banker says, 'out of every dollar we earned abroad, eighty cents was pure surplus. A surplus provided by the land – the rain, the climate, the earth.' The land might be said to be Indian land, but the Indians had been exterminated in the nineteenth century. A monument in the Prado park commemorates Uruguay's last four Charrua Indians, who were sent as exhibits to the Musée de l'Homme in Paris, where they died.

Pensions, every kind of worker's benefit, women's rights: month after month Batlle handed down the liberal laws to an astonished pastoral people. And suddenly Uruguay was modern, the best-educated country in South America, with the most liberal laws; and Montevideo was a metropolis, full of statues.

Sábat, the cartoonist, who left Uruguay eight years

ago and now works in Buenos Aires, says: 'Uruguay is a big *estancia*. Only a megalomaniac like Batlle could think that it was a country. It remains a big *estancia* with a city, Montevideo, that is crystallized on the 1930s. Creativity stopped then. The country was developing intellectually. After Batlle everything was *crystallized*.'

The socialist teacher, more romantic, grieves for the gaucho past. 'Batlle should not have been born in a bucolic country. He went to Europe and got all those lovely ideas and then looked around for a country where he could apply them. And as the country didn't exist he invented it. He invented the industrial worker, bringing in people from the country to the town. People used to drinking maté, watching sheep, sitting under the ombú tree – which wasn't bad, you know: it was beautiful: the twentieth century doesn't want us to live like that. He invented the workers and then he invented the social laws and then the bureaucracy – which was terrible. I am not certain why this should have led to corruption and venality, but it did.'

The businessman: 'Utopia is the worst thing for a man. He is old at thirty. That happened to us.'

The banker: 'All the productive infrastructure was built between 1850 and 1930 and was based on existing British investments. Very little was done afterwards. A power plant was finished after 1945; that was the most important addition. No new roads, no new bridges. The country was living like a retired person on a pension.'

And with the new state, a new glory. Football, introduced by British railway workers, became the Uruguayan obsession. Sábat: 'Our provincialism was backed up by our football – a proof of greatness that had no relation with reality. In 1924 in Paris and in 1928 in Amsterdam we were the Olympic champions. We were the world champions in Montevideo in 1930 and in Rio in 1950. And we thought: If we are world champions in football, then we must be world champions in everything.'

In the park named after Batlle, the great football stadium, built in 1930 (together with the Legislative Palace) for the centenary of Uruguay's independence, and named after Batlle, still draws the crowds. The newspapers still devote half their news space to football. But football has decayed with the economy; and now, like the cattle, the better footballers have to be sold off to richer countries as soon as they are reared.

There are many jokes in Uruguay about the bureaucracy; and they all are true. Out of a workforce of just over a million, 250,000 are employed by the state. PLUNA, the Uruguayan airline, used to have one thousand employees and one functioning airplane. The people at ANCAP, the state oil company, tried to get to the office before it opened: there were more employees than chairs.

In 1958 the Ministry of Public Health recruited fifteen hundred new staff. In 1959 in Public Works there was one messenger for every six civil servants. In Telephones and Electricity there are forty-five grades of civil servants. Nothing is done by post; everything requires a personal visit. The service is slow; but the public, scattered among the messengers and the sleeping police dogs in the foyer, is uncomplaining: many of them are civil servants from other departments, with time on their hands.

It is a kind of ideal: government offices that are like clubs for public and staff, a whole country living the life of a commune, work and leisure flowering together, everyone, active and inactive, a pensioner of the state. But Uruguay still lives off meat and wool; and Montevideo, which contains more than a third of the country's population, is an artificial metropolis. The padding of the civil service, which began thirty years ago, in the time of wealth, disguises unemployement and urban purposelessness. Everyone knows this, but too many people benefit: the whole state has been led into this conspiracy against itself. 'Everyone is pension-minded,' the businessman says. And even the left-wing slogans of protest against the military government can be cautious and practical: *Paz Salario Libertad*: Peace Wages Liberty.

The girls in blue nylon coats in Telephones and Electricity earn about 120 dollars a month. In summer, from December to March, they work from seven to one. They go off then to a second job. Or they go to the beach. Montevideo is built along a beach; all roads south end in white sand and a bay.

And this is where Uruguayans regularly lose all sense of crisis, and the will to action is weakened: on the too accessible beach, in the resort developments just a few minutes outside Montevideo where many modest people have summer houses amid pines and dunes, and in Punta del Este, one of Uruguay's economic disasters, built mainly in the 1950s with loans from the Mortgage Bank, the satellite resort town of the artificial metropolis.

Everyone rejects Batllismo, but after sixty years everyone in Uruguay has been made by it. The resort life is all they know; its crumbling away leaves them confused. 'Spiritually,' the journalist said, 'we feel we have gone back.' Spiritually? 'I don't like to be stressed permanently.' He was a two-house man; but he had to do two jobs, one with the government; and his wife was doing two jobs. And cars were expensive, because of the 300 per cent tax. A new Volkswagen cost 8,000 dollars; even a 1955 Rover cost 3,500 dollars. 'We won't progress. What's progress, though. America? That's consuming and stressing, keeping up with the Joneses. We don't have that kind of shit here, if you pardon the expression.'

But there was the high price of cars.

'I'll tell you about Uruguay in one sentence,' the architect said to me on my first evening in Montevideo. 'The last Jaguar was imported in 1955.'

These are withdrawal symptoms and they add up to a

kind of spiritual distress: Montevideo, spreading along its beach, needs the motorcar. Without the motorcar, tracts of the city will have to be abandoned, as the Prado park has been abandoned. All that resort life, all that modernity of which the Uruguayans were until recently so proud, depends on consumer goods which Uruguay bought from more 'stressed' countries and – wasting the talent of two generations in a padded civil service – never learned to make.

The antique cars of Montevideo – pre-1955 Citroëns, baby Morrises and Austins, Fords and Chevrolets of the 1930s, and other names now abandoned or superseded: Hupmobile, Willys-Overland Whippet, Dodge Brothers, Hudson – are not as gay as they first appear, part of the resort life. The country is under siege. The simplest things are smuggled in by lorry from Argentina; the supplies of modern civilization are running out.

Uruguayans say that they are a European nation, that they have always had their back to the rest of South America. It was their great error, and is part of their failure. Their habits of wealth made them, profoundly a colonial people, educated but intellectually null, consumers, parasitic on the culture and technology of others.

The Tupamaros were destroyers. They had no programme; they were like people provoking a reaction, challenging the hidden enemy to declare himself. In the end they picked on the armed forces and were speedily destroyed. 'The Tupamaros were not the beginning of a revolution,' Sábat says. 'They were the last whisper of Batllismo. They were parricides, engaged in a kind of kamikaze. In Uruguay now, everybody, whatever slogans he shouts, is either a parricide or a reactionary.'

There is no middle way. Political attitudes have grown simpler and harder; and it is impossible not to take sides. On the last Saturday in October a student in the engineering faculty of the university blew himself up while

135

making a bomb. The army closed the university – independent until that day – and arrested everybody. Parricide or reactionary, left-wing or right-wing, each side now finds in the other the enemy he needs. Each side now assigns a destructive role to the other; and, as in Chile, people grow into their roles.

Those who can, get out. They queue for passports at the rear entrance of the pink-walled Foreign Ministry, formerly the Santos Palace (built in 1880, the basin of the fountain in the hall carved from a single block of Carrara marble). In October there were reports of people queueing all night. At Carrasco Airport the other day someone chalked on a wall: *'El último que salga que apague la luz'*: 'The last person to leave must put out the light'.

4   The Brothels Behind the Graveyard

May–July 1974

The prophecy – according to some old Argentine book of prophecies, which I often heard about but never saw – was that Perón would be hanged by his followers in the Plaza de Mayo, the main square in downtown Buenos Aires. But Perón died with his legend intact. 'M U R I O': 'He is dead.' The headline filled half the front page of *Crónica*, a popular Buenos Aires newspaper; and there was no need to give the name.

He was in his seventy-ninth year and in the ninth month of his third presidential term; and his legend had lasted for nearly thirty years. He was the army man who had moved out of the code of his caste and shaken up the old colonial agricultural society of Argentina; he had identified the enemies of the poor; he had created the trade unions. He had given a brutal face to the brutish land of *estancias* and polo and brothels and very cheap servants. And his legend, as the unique revolutionary, survived the incompetence and plunder of his early rule; it survived his overthrow in 1955 and the seventeen years of exile that followed; it survived the mob killings that attended his triumphant return last year; and it survived the failure of his last months in office.

The failure was obvious. Perón could not control the Argentina he had called into being twenty years before. He had identified the cruelties of the society, and yet he had made that necessary task seem irresponsible: he had not been able to reorganize the society he had undermined. And perhaps that task of reorganization was beyond the capacities of any leader, however creative. Politics reflect a society and a land. Argentina is a land of plunder, a new land, virtually peopled in this century. It remains a land to be plundered; and its politics can be nothing but the politics of plunder.

Everyone in Argentina understands and accepts this, and in the end Perón could only offer himself as a guarantee of his government's purpose, could only offer his words. In the end he had become his name alone, a presence, above it all, above the people who acted in his name, above the inflation and the shortages and the further steep decline of the peso, the faction fights, the daily kidnappings and guerrilla shootouts, the strong rumours of plunder in high places: above the Argentina whose brutality and frenzies he had divined and exploited, the Argentina he had returned to save, and which he now leaves behind him.

He was very old, and perhaps his cause had become more personal than he knew: to return to his homeland and to be rehabilitated. He made his peace with the armed forces, who had previously stripped him of his rank. He made his peace with the Church, against whom, in his second term, he had warred: he was to die holding the rosary given him by Pope Paul. He came back from exile a softened man, even philosophical, with ideas about ecology and the environment and the unity of Latin America ('By 2000 we shall be united or dominated'). But these ideas were remote from the anxieties of his followers and the power conflicts of the country. And towards the end he seemed to have recognized that the country was beyond his control.

Two years ago, when the military still ruled, everyone was Peronist, even Maoist priests and Trotskyist guerrillas. Perón, or his name, united all who wanted to see an end to military rule. But, inevitably, when Perón began to rule, it became necessary to distinguish the true Peronists from the 'infiltrators'. And the man who had returned as a national leader, as the 'conductor' of all the warring elements of the movement that carried his name, began once again, like the old Perón, to detect enemies. There were enemies on the Left, among the guerrilla groups who had helped to bring him back to power. There were enemies on the Right. So many people were seen, as the months passed, 'sabotaging the current political process'. Week by week the semi-official *El Caudillo* identified new enemies. So many enemies: towards the end it was possible to detect in Perón's words the helpless, aggrieved tone of his writings after his overthrow in 1955.

On June 10th, Perón's wife, the Vice-President, in a speech printed the next day in full-page advertisements in the newspapers, spoke of the speculators and hoarders and other 'executioners of the nation' who were responsible for the shortages and the high prices. Perón couldn't do it all, she said; and she wondered whether the country wasn't failing Perón. On June 11th, Perón's former secretary, companion and soothsayer, López Rega, now Minister for Social Welfare, spoke more clearly. He told a group of provincial governors: 'If General Perón leaves the country before his mission is accomplished, he won't be going alone. His wife will go with him, and your humble servant [*este servidor*].'

Perón, Rega said, couldn't do it all, and he shouldn't be expected to. 'The philosophy of Justicialism isn't only a matter of shouting *Viva Perón*. It means taking to heart the meaning of this philosophy, which is simply that we should all, without question, comply with the objectives of greatness and fulfilment so that we might have a happy nation.' Meaningless words – the translation is the best I can do; but after the identification of enemies, it was perhaps the only way Peronism could be defined.

The wife had spoken, the secretary had spoken. The next day Perón himself spoke. Abruptly, at a meeting where he had been expected to talk of other things, he announced that he was fed up and disheartened, and that if he didn't get more cooperation he was willing to hand over the government to people who thought they could do better.

The trade unions responded immediately. They asked their members to stop work. In the Córdoba Hills, where I was, the bus drivers didn't even know what it was all about or where the action was; they only knew, strike-hardened union men, that the buses weren't going to run after midday. The action, as it turned out, was confined to Buenos Aires, where in the Plaza de Mayo a great union rally was swiftly conjured up. Perón addressed the rally and received their applause; he pronounced himself satisfied, and it was assumed that he wasn't after all going to leave the country to stew in its own juice. The whole cabinet resigned that evening; one or two ministers gave grave interviews. It seemed at least that some treachery was going to be exposed and that some heads were going to roll. But no heads rolled; the whole cabinet was reappointed.

It was a curious event: so well prepared, so dramatic in its effect, and then entirely without sequel. The newspapers, full of crisis one day, reporting the entire republic in a state of tension, the next day quietly forgot about it. Newspapers are like that in Argentina. It was

Perón's last demagogic act, his last political flourish. And no one will know what, if anything, lay behind it, whether illness and death put an end to some new development, something that was going to make clear the purpose and plans of the new government. It was what people were waiting for. No one knew what was happening in Argentina; and some people were beginning to feel that there might be nothing to know.

The mystery isn't the mystery of Perón alone, but of Argentina, where the political realities, of plunder and the animosities engendered by plunder, have for so long been clouded by rhetoric. The rhetoric fools no one. But in a country where government has never been open and intellectual resources are scant, the rhetoric of a regime is usually all that survives to explain it. Argentina has the apparatus of an educated, open society. There are newspapers and magazines and universities and publishing houses; there is even a film industry. But the country has as yet no idea of itself. Streets and avenues are named after presidents and generals, but there is no art of historical analysis; there is no art of biography. There is legend and antiquarian romance, but no real history. There are only annals, lists of rulers, chronicles of events.

The sharpest political commentator in Argentina is Mariano Grondona. He appears on television, and is said to be of a good Argentine family. At the end of May, *Gente*, a popular illustrated weekly, interviewed Grondona and asked him to analyse the events of the past year: the year of the disintegration of Peronism as a national movement, the year of the detection and casting out of enemies. *Gente* considered Grondona's views important enough to be spread over five pages.

To understand Argentine history, Grondona said, it was necessary to break it up into epochs, *épocas*. Since independence in 1810 there had been seven epochs. Seven republics, almost: Argentina had to be seen as having a French-style history, a Latin history. The Latin mentality worked from principles; it exhausted one set of principles and moved through upheaval to a new set. Anglo-Saxons, more pragmatic, didn't define their principles. They were therefore spared periods of chaos; but at the same time they didn't enjoy 'those magnificent moments in which everything is remade', *'esos instantes magníficos en que todo recomienza'*.

The fifth epoch of Argentine history, from 1945 to 1955, was the epoch of Peronism. The sixth epoch, from 1955 to 1973, was the military epoch, the epoch of the exclusion of Peronism. The seventh epoch, beginning in 1973, was the epoch of revived institutions, the epoch of the return of Peronism. This last epoch, though only a year old, had been confusing; but it would be less so if it were divided into *etapas*, stages. Perón, like Mao, lived 'in stages'. Peronism had first to pass through a 'smiling' stage, when it was looking for power, then an embattled stage, when it was fighting for power, and then an apparently established stage, when it had achieved power. A number of Peronists had remained stuck at the second, embattled stage; that was why they had to be got rid of.

There is no question, in Grondona's analysis, of people either acting badly or being badly treated. The people who had come to grief during the Peronist year simply hadn't understood this Argentine business of *épocas* and *etapas*. Some of them had got their *etapas* badly mixed up – like the dentist who had become President as Perón's nominee, but had then been deemed a traitor and dismissed.

Other difficult events of the year became clearer once it was understood that an *etapa* itself consisted of great days, *jornadas*; and there were *jornadas*, apparently chaotic, that could be broken up into phases, *fases*. 'We are accustomed to this pattern of *épocas* and *jornadas* ... There will be other epochs and other great days. I am convinced of that. All that we can ask of this one is that it should fulfil its historical duty.'

This is how Grondona ends, fitting a sentence of Argentine rhetoric to an account of a year's murderous power struggle. To the outsider, Grondona, with his nimbleness and zest, is curiously detached: he might be speaking of a country far away. It is hard to imagine, from his account, that people are still being killed and kidnapped in the streets, or that in June the army was fighting guerrillas in Tucumán, or that newspapers, under the general heading '*Guerrillerismo*', carry reports of the previous day's guerrilla happenings. There is detachment and an unconscious cynicism in Grondona's chronicle. The political life of the country is seen as little more than a struggle for political power. There seems to be no higher good. And – what is more alarming, more revealing of Argentina – the chronicle is offered to the readers of *Gente* as to people who know no higher good.

So Perón and his legend pass into the annals. The legend is admired now; in time it will almost certainly be reviled. But the legend itself will not alter: it will be all that people will have to go by. It is how history is written in Argentina. And perhaps a people who had learned to read their history in another way, who had ceased to accept the politics of plunder, might have spared themselves the futility of the last year of Perón.

But the history, as it is written, is of a piece with the politics. And the politics reflect the people and the land. There are Argentines who feel that their country deserved better than Perón. They feel that their country was ridiculed and diminished by the Peronist court rule of the last year: Perón the derelict macho, Isabelita his consort and Vice-President, López Rega the powerful secretary-soothsayer – sultan, sultana and grand vizier.

But Perón was what he was because he touched Argentina so closely. He intuited the needs of his followers: where he appeared to violate, there he usually triumphed.

He went too far when he made war on the Church in his second presidential term; but that was his only error as a people's leader. He brought out and made strident the immigrant proletarian reality of a country where, in the women's magazines, the myth still reigns of 'old' families and polo and romance down at the *estancia*. He showed the country its unacknowledged half-Indian face. And by imposing his women on Argentina, first Evita and then Isabelita, one an actress, the other a cabaret dancer, both provincials, by turning women branded as the macho's easy victims into the macho's rulers, he did the roughest kind of justice on a society still ruled by a degenerate machismo, which decrees that a woman's place is essentially in the brothel.

Still, it remains odd about Perón: he spoke so much about the greatness of the country, but in himself, and in his movement, he expressed so many of his country's weaknesses and revealed them as irremediable.

The aeroplane, coming down to land at Ezeiza Airport outside Buenos Aires, flies over the green land of Uruguay, once so rich and now, like Argentina, a land of disorder and sorrow; and then over the wide, chocolate-coloured estuary of the Río de la Plata. Quite abruptly on the tawny flat land south of the estuary the white and grey buildings of Buenos Aires are seen to arise: a city of inexplicable size that seems arbitrarily sited at the very edge of an empty continent, along that expanse of muddy water. The aeroplane shows it all: the great estuary, the sudden city of eight million, the outer rim of the vast, flat, empty hinterland – the simple geography of a remote southern land with a simple history of Indian genocide and European takeover. Not resettlement: resettlement would have created a smaller city, might have peopled and humanized the Indian hinterland.

There is as yet in Argentina no myth of the noble Indian. The memory of the genocide is too close; it is still something to be dismissed in a line or two in the annals. In Argentina the detestation of the vanished pampa Indian is instinctive and total: the Argentine terror is that people in other countries might think of Argentina as an Indian country. Borges, who is very old, has often told his foreign interviewers that the Indians of Argentina couldn't count. And to a forty-year-old artist of my acquaintance, the pampa Indians were 'like grass'.

From the great town, highways push out in all directions through the once-Indian hinterland. The town dies hard; low, boxlike brick houses straggle beside the highways for miles. At last the land is clear; and very quickly, then, the flatness of the pampa, the height of sky, the distances and the emptiness numb response. No trees grew here. But in the unused rich soil trees grow fast now, and occasionally tall eucalyptus trees screen a park and a big house. The land is full of military names, the names of generals who took the land away from the Indians and, with a rapacity that still outrages the imagination, awarded themselves great portions of the earth's surface, estates, *estancias*, as large as counties.

It was the time of the great imperialist push in many continents. While President Roca was systematically exterminating the Indians, the Belgians were opening up their brand-new Congo. Joseph Conrad saw the Belgians at work, and in *Heart of Darkness* he catches their frenzy. 'Their talk was the talk of sordid buccaneers; it was reckless without hardihood, greedy without audacity, and cruel without courage; there was not an atom of foresight or of serious intention in the whole batch of them, and they did not seem aware these things are wanted for the work of the world.' The words fit the Argentine frenzy; they contain the mood and the moral nullity of that Argentine enterprise which have worked down through the generations to the failure of today.

The great private domains have split, but the *estancias* are still very big. The scale is still superhuman. The *estan-*

cias are mechanized and require little labour; the landscape remains empty and unhumanized. There are little towns, sitting fragilely on the pampa, but they provide only the bare necessities: the stupefying nightclub, which enables people who have said everything already to be together for hours without saying anything; the brothel, which simplifies the world even further; the garage. Away from the highways there is a sense of desolation. The dirt roads are wide and straight; trees are few; and the flat land stretches uninterrupted to the horizon. The sense of distance is distorted: things miles away seem close – an *estancia* workman on horseback, a clump of trees, a junction of dirt roads. The desolation would be complete without the birds; and they, numerous, unusually big, and gaudily coloured, emphasize the alienness of the land and the fewness of men. Every morning on the pampa highways there are dead brown owls.

The land here is something to be worked. It is not a thing of beauty; it has not been hallowed by the cinema, literature or art, or by the life of rooted communities. Land in Argentina, as I heard a South American banker from another country say, is still only a commodity. It is an investment, a hedge against inflation. It can be alienated without heartache. Argentina's wealth is in the land; this land explains the great city on the estuary. But the land has become no one's home. Home is elsewhere: Buenos Aires, England, Italy, Spain. You can live in Argentina, many Argentines say, only if you can leave.

The Argentina created by the railways and President Roca's Remingtons still has the structure and purpose of a colony. And, oddly, in the manner of its founding and in its implied articles of association, it is like a sixteenth-century colony of the Spanish Empire, with the same greed and internal weaknesses, the same potential for dissension, the cynicism and sterility. *Obedezco pero no cumplo*, I obey but I don't comply: it was the attitude of the sixteenth-century conquistador or official, who had a contract with the King of Spain alone, and not with the King's other subjects. In Argentina the contract is not with other Argentines, but with the rich land, the precious commodity. This is how it was in the beginning and how, inevitably, it continues to be.

There is no king (though Perón was that, the man in whose name everyone acted). But there is a flag (the colours, blue and white, honour a saint, but Argentines are taught that they are the colours of their sky). And people who feel that the land has failed them wave the flag: the workers in the cities, the young men in new suits, immigrants' sons who have become doctors or lawyers. But this patriotism is less than it appears. In Argentina, unmade, flawed from its conception, without a history, still only with annals, there can be no feeling for a past, for a heritage, for shared ideals, for a community of all Argentines. Every Argentine wants to ratify his own contract with the God-given land, miraculously cleansed of Indians and still empty.

There are many Argentinas, and they all exist within that idea of the richness of the land. In the north-west there is an older Argentina, settled by Spaniards spreading down south from Peru. At the foot of the Cordilleras is the city of La Rioja, founded nearly four hundred years ago by a Spaniard looking for gold. It is distinctive; its people are of the land, and half Indian. It has a completeness not found in the cities of the newer Argentina, from which it is separated by the waterless flat wilderness of the *llanos*, bisected to the very horizon, as it seems to the passenger in a bus, by the straight black road, whose edges are blurred by drifting sand.

But at the end of that road, and among the Córdoba Hills, where imported cypress and willow create irregular little Mediterranean patches on the barren hillsides, there is an English-style boarding school, recently founded. It is successful and well equipped; the headmaster, when I saw him, had just stocked the library with an expensive uniform set of the world's best books.

The school might seem an anachronism, the headmaster says; but the aim isn't to create English gentlemen; it is to create gentlemen for Argentina. There is rugger on Sunday morning. A school from Córdoba is visiting, and the school servants are grilling thick thongs of red meat over an enormous barbecue pit. 'Just like Anglo-Saxons to make up a game like rugger,' says the young teacher, fresh from the constrictions of London, and flourishing in the atmosphere of freedom and fantasy which the emptiness of Argentina can so agreeably suggest to people who have just arrived.

At the local church the elderly British residents, retired people, had that morning prayed for both Perón and the Queen. The previous evening they had gathered at a hotel to see the film of Princess Anne's wedding.

Half an hour away by bus there is an Italo-Spanish peasant town: low houses, cracked plaster, exposed red bricks, pollarded trees, dust, Mediterranean colours, women in black, girls and children in doorways. Water is scarce. There is a big dam, but it was breached two years ago. The people grow cotton and olives and consider their town rich.

The ten-hour bus drive from the industrial town of Córdoba, where they make motorcars, to the city of La Rioja is like a drive through many countries, many eras, many fading ancestral cultures. The ancestral culture fades, and Argentina offers no substitute. It offers only the land, the cheap food and the cheap wine. To all those people on the road from Córdoba to La Rioja it offers accommodation, and what had once seemed a glorious freedom. To none does it offer a country. They are, by an unlikely irony, among the last victims of imperialism, and not just in the way Perón said.

*

Argentina is a simple materialist society, a simple colonial society created in the most rapacious and decadent phase of imperialism. It has diminished and stultified the men whom it attracted by the promise of ease and to whom it offered no other ideals and no new idea of human association. New Zealand, equally colonial, also with a past of native dispossession, but founded at an earlier imperial period and on different principles, has had a different history. It has made some contribution to the world; more gifted men and women have come from its population of three million than from the twenty-three millions of Argentines.

Two years ago, when I was new to Argentina, an academic said to me, during the Buenos Aires rush hour: 'You would think you were in a developed country.' It wasn't easy then to understand his irony and bitterness. Buenos Aires is such an overwhelming metropolis that it takes time to understand that it is new and has been imported almost whole; that its metropolitan life is an illusion, a colonial mimicry; that it feeds on other countries and is itself sterile. The great city was intended as the servant of its hinterland and it was set down, complete, on the edge of the continent. Its size was not dictated by its own needs nor did it reflect its own excellence. Buenos Aires, from the nature of its creation, has never required excellence: that has always been one of its attractions. Within the imported metropolis there is the structure of a developed society. But men can often appear to be mimicking their functions. So many words have acquired lesser meanings in Argentina: *general, artist, journalist, historian, professor, university, director, executive, industrialist, aristocrat, library, museum, zoo*; so many words need inverted commas. To write realistically about this society has peculiar difficulties; to render it accurately in fiction might be impossible.

For men so diminished there remains only machismo. There is the machismo of the football field or the racing track. And there is machismo as simple stylishness: the police motorcyclist, for instance, goggled and gloved, weaving about at speed, siren going, clearing a path for the official car. But machismo is really about the conquest and humiliation of women. In the sterile society it is the victimization, by the simple, of the simpler. Women in Argentina are uneducated and have few rights; they are reared either for early marriage or for domestic service. Very few have money or the means of earning money. They are meant to be victims; and they accept their victim role.

Machismo makes no man stand out, because every man is assumed to be a macho. Sexual conquest is a duty. It has little to do with passion or even attraction; and conquests are not achieved through virility or any special skills. In a society so ruled by the idea of plunder, the macho's attractions, from the top to the bottom of the money scale, are essentially economic. Clothes, reflecting the macho's wealth or 'class', are an important sexual signal. So is the wallet. And the macho's keys, symbols of property, have to be displayed. The symbolism is crude; but the society isn't subtle. The bus driver, a small-time macho, hangs his two keys from his belt over his right hip; the right hip of the 'executive' can be positively encased in metal, with the keys hanging from the belt by heavy metal loops. Money makes the macho. Machismo requires, and imposes, a widespread amateur prostitution; it is a society spewing on itself.

The thing has been institutionalized; and the institution is served by a gigantic brothel industry. There are brothels everywhere, open night and day. Enormous new buildings, their function proclaimed by neon signs and a general garishness, are strung along the Pan American Highway. In the heart of the city, behind the Recoleta Cemetery, where the illustrious are buried, there is an avenue of tall brothels. The brothels charge by the hour. In the dim lobby of such a place a red spotlight might

149

play on a crude bronze-coloured woman's bust: the bad art of Argentina. Every schoolgirl knows the brothels; from an early age she understands that she might have to go there one day to find love, among the coloured lights and mirrors.

The act of straight sex, easily bought, is of no great moment to the macho. His conquest of a woman is complete only when he has buggered her. This is what the woman has it in her power to deny; this is what the brothel game is about, the passionless Latin adventure that begins with talk of *amor*. *La tuve en el culo*, I've had her in the arse: this is how the macho reports victory to his circle, or dismisses a desertion. Contemporary sexologists give a general dispensation to buggery. But the buggering of women is of special significance in Argentina and other Latin American countries. The Church considers it a heavy sin, and prostitutes hold it in horror. By imposing on her what prostitutes reject, and what he knows to be a kind of sexual black mass, the Argentine macho, in the main of Spanish or Italian peasant ancestry, consciously dishonours his victim. So diminished men, turning to machismo, diminish themselves further, replacing even sex by a parody.

The cartoonist Sábat, in some of his Grosz-like drawings, has hinted at the diseased, half-castrated nature of machismo. In Buenos Aires the other day a new film opened and was a great success: *Boquitas Pintadas – Little Painted Mouths* – made by Argentina's most famous director and based on a novel by an Argentine writer, Manuel Puig. The film – clumsy and overacted and without polish – is the story of the life and death of a tubercular small-town macho. An aimless film, it seemed, a real-life chronicle on which no pattern had been imposed. But the Argentine audience wept: for them the tragedy lay in the foreseeable death of the macho, the poor boy of humble family who made his conquests the hard way, by his beauty.

To the outsider the tragedy lay elsewhere, in the apparent motivelessness of so much of the action. No relationship was hinted at, and no comment seemed to be offered by writer or director: it was as though, in the society of machismo, the very knowledge of the possibility of deeper relationships had been lost. After the macho's death one of his women had a dream: in bleached colour, and in very slow motion, the macho rose from his grave, in his pretty macho clothes, lifted her in his arms, flew with her through a bedroom window and placed her on a bed. On this necrophiliac fantasy the film ended. And the audience was in tears.

To go outside after this, to walk past the long queue for the film, to see the lights of packed cafés and bars, the young people in flared jeans, was to have the sharpest sense of the mimicry and alienness of the great city. It was to have a sense of the incompleteness and degeneracy of these transplanted people who seemed so whole, to begin to understand and fear their violence, their peasant cruelty, their belief in magic, and their fascination with death, celebrated every day in the newspapers with pictures of murdered people, often guerrilla victims, lying in their coffins.

After the genocide, a great part of our earth is being turned into a wasteland. The failure of Argentina, so rich, so underpopulated, twenty-three million people in a million square miles, is one of the mysteries of our time. Commentators like Mariano Grondona, unravelling chaos, tying themselves up in *etapas*, will try to make sense of irrational acts and inconsequential events by talking of Argentina's French-style history. Others will offer political explanations and suggest poltical remedies. But politics have to do with the nature of human association, the contract of men with men. The politics of a country can only be an extension of its idea of human relationships.

151

Perón, in himself, as folk leader, expressed many of his country's weaknesses. And it is necessary to look where he, the greatest macho of them all (childless and reportedly impotent), pointed: to the centre of Buenos Aires and to those tall brothels, obscenely shuttered, that stand, suitably, behind the graveyard.

5   The Terror

March 1977

In Argentina the killer cars – the cars in which the official gunmen go about their business – are Ford Falcons. The Falcon, which is made in Argentina, is a sturdy small car of unremarkable appearance, and there are thousands on the roads. But the killer Falcons are easily recognizable. They have no number plates. The cars – and the plainclothesmen they carry – require to be noticed; and people can sometimes stand and watch.

As they stood and watched some weeks ago, in the main square of the northern city of Tucumán: the Falcons parked in the semicircular drive of Government Headquarters, an ornate stone building like a nineteenth-century European country house, but with Indian soldiers with machine guns on the balcony and in the well-kept subtropical gardens: a glimpse, eventually, of uniforms, handshakes, salutes, until the men in plain clothes, like actors impersonating an aristocratic shooting party, but with machine guns under their Burberrys or imitation Burberrys, came down the wide steps, got into the small cars and drove off without speed or sirens.

The authorities have grown to understand the dramatic effect of silence. It is part of the terror that is meant to be felt as terror.

Style is important in Argentina; and in the long-running guerrilla war – in spite of the real blood, the real torture – there has always been an element of machismo and public theatre. In the old days policemen stood a little way from busy intersections with machine guns at the ready; at night the shopping streets of central Buenos Aires were patrolled by jackbooted and helmeted soldiers with Alsatian dogs; from time to time, as a dramatic extravaganza, there appeared the men of the anti-guerrilla motorcycle brigade. The war in those days was in the main a private war, between the guerrillas on one side and the army and police on the other. Now the war touches everybody; public theatre has turned to public terror.

Style has been taken away from all but the men in the Falcons. The guerrillas still operate, but the newspapers are not allowed to print anything about them. They can print only the repetitive official communiqués, the body counts, and these usually appear as small items on the inside pages, seemingly unrelated to the rest of the news: in such a place, on such a date, in these circumstances, so many subversives or *delincuentes* were killed, so many men, so many women. The communiqués are thought to represent only a fraction of the truth: too many people are disappearing.

In the beginning – after the chaos and near-anarchy of the Peronist restoration – the killings were thought to be good for the economy. War was war, it was said; the guerrillas – now like private armies, with no recognizable aims – had to be rooted out; the trade unions and their leaders had to be disciplined after the licence and corruption of the Peronist years. (No more free trips to Europe on Aerolíneas Argentinas for those union men, flashy provincial machos requiring attention from the crew, each man, after supper, settling down with his pile of comic books and photo-novels, light reading for the long night flights, the tips of ringed fingers wetted on the tongue before the pages were turned.) Another, more becoming, Argentina was to be created; the country (as though the country were an economic abstraction, something that could be separated from the bulk of the population) was to be got going again.

And while wages were kept down like sin, the banker-saints of Argentina worked their own inflationary miracles. They offered 8 per cent a month or 144 per cent a year for the peso, and momentarily gave back faith to many good Argentines who had for years been praying only for the water of their pesos to be turned into the wine of dollars. During the early months of the terror the stock market boomed; fortunes were made out of nothing; Argentina seemed to be itself again. But now – even with that 144 per cent – the terror is too close.

No pattern can any longer be discerned in the terror. It isn't only the guerrillas and the union men and the country's few intellectuals who are threatened. Anyone can be picked up. Torture is routine. Even workmen unlucky enough to be in a flat at the time of a raid have been taken away, held for a few hours and tortured with everybody else, so automatic is the process: the tight blindfold, the eyes depressed in the sockets, the hooding, the beating, the electric shocks that leave burn marks for eighteen days, and then the mysterious journey in the boot of the Falcon and the sadism of release: 'We are taking you to the cemetery ... Now, count a hundred before you take off your blindfold.'

Almost everyone in Argentina now knows someone who has disappeared or been arrested or tortured. Even military men have, by the intervention of military friends, been called to receive the corpses of their children, corpses which might otherwise have been destroyed or thrown away, sometimes to roll ashore, mutilated and decomposing, at Montevideo, on the other side of the Río de la Plata. One woman was sent the hands of her daughter in a shoe box.

There is still, for the distinguished or well known,

legal arrest on specific charges. But below that there is no law. People are taken away and no one is responsible. The army refers inquirers to the police, and the police refer them back to the army. A special language has developed: an anxious father might be told that his son's case is 'closed'. No one really knows who does what or why; it is said that anyone can now be made to disappear, for a price.

Buenos Aires is full of shocked and damaged people who can think now only of flight, who find it no longer possible to take sides, who can see no cause in Argentina and can acknowledge at last the barbarism by which they have for long been surrounded, the barbarism they had previously been content to balance against the knowledge of their own security and the old Argentine lure of the spacious rich land, easy money and abundant meat, the lure expressed in the words that so often in Argentina close a discussion: *'Todavia aqui se vive mejor.'* 'Still, you live better here.'

Barbarism, in a city which has thought of itself as European, in a land which, because of that city, has prided itself on its civilization. Barbarism because of that very idea: civilization felt as something far away, magically kept going by others: the civilization of Europe divorced from any idea of an intellectual life and equated with the goods and fashions of Europe: civilization felt as something purchasable, something always there, across the ocean, for the man or woman with enough money: an attitude not far removed from that of the politician of a new country who, while fouling his own nest, feathers another abroad, in a land of law.

The official history of Argentina is a history of glory: of a war of independence, with heroes, of European expansion, wealth, civilization. This is the past of which Borges sometimes sings; but a recurring theme of some of his later stories is of cultural degeneracy.

*

Torture is not new in Argentina. And though Argen-
times abroad, when they are campaigning against a particular regime, talk as if torture has just been started by
that regime, in Argentina itself torture is spoken of – and
accepted – by all groups as an Argentine institution.

In 1972, at an elegant provincial hotel, an upper-class
lady of Spanish descent (still obsessed with the purity of
race, still fighting the old Spanish wars) told me that
torture had started in Argentina in 1810, when the
country became independent of Spain; and – middle-
aged and delicate at the dinner table, drinking the yellow
champagne of Argentina, and speaking English with the
accent of the finishing school – she said that torture remained necessary because the penal code was so benign.
'You have to kill a man in the most horrible way to go to
gaol. "My client was excited," the lawyer says. "Oh?" the
judge says. "He was excited?" And no gaol.'

A young Trotskyist lawyer didn't see the law quite like
that. He thought only that torture had been used by
'most of the governments' and had become 'a pretty important feature of Argentine life'. Its abolition seemed
at first to form no part of his socialist programme; but
then, noticing my concern, he promised, speaking very
quickly, as to a child to whom anything could be promised, that torture would disappear 'with the downfall
of the bourgeoisie'.

However, the high Peronist trade union man I later
went to see – this was in mid-1972, and the union man
was close to power, waiting for Perón to come back –
couldn't promise anything. He said – and he might have
been speaking of rain – that torture would always exist.
It was this man, soft-voiced, reasonable, at that time still
the representative of the oppressed, who told me – the
map of the Paris metro and a photograph of the young
Perón below glass on his desk – that there was good
torture and bad torture. It was 'all right' to torture an
'evildoer'; it was another thing to torture 'a man who's
trying to serve the country'.

And that was the very point made four years later by Admiral Guzzetti, one of the leaders of the present regime, when, defending the terror, he spoke to the United Nations in August 1976. The Admiral (who has since been wounded in a guerrilla attack) said: 'My idea of subversion is that of the left-wing terrorist organizations. Subversion or terrorism of the right is not the same thing. When the social body of the country has been contaminated by a disease that corrodes its entrails, it forms antibodies. These antibodies cannot be considered in the same way as the microbes.'

Yesterday's antibodies, today's microbes; yesterday's servants of the country, today's evildoers; yesterday's torturers, today's tortured. Argentine ideologies, in spite of the labels of Right or Left that they give themselves, are really quite simple. What harms the other man is right; what harms me is wrong. Perón was never more Argentine – in his complaints and his moral outrage – than when, in 1956, the year after he had been overthrown by the military, he published his own lachrymose account of the affair. He called his book *La Fuerza Es el Derecho de las Bestias*. The words mean, literally, 'Force is the right of animals', and the title might be rendered in English as *The Law of the Jungle*.

In that book Perón wrote: 'The revolution is without a cause because it is only a reaction. It seeks only to undo what has been done, to extirpate Peronism, to take away from the workers the benefits they have won.' And Perón, if he were alive today, might use the same words about the present regime. So little has Argentina changed in the political seesawing of the last twenty years; so without point have been all the manoeuvrings and murders.

The killer cars are not new. They began to operate in Perón's time, when Perón turned against the guerrillas who had brought him back to power. And the cars became more murderous in the time of Isabel, Perón's widow and successor, when the enemies became more personal, less politically definable. Then one day Isabel ceased to rule, and the Peronist cycle was over.

It happened simply. Late one evening the military, who had held off for a long time, had the presidential helicopter hijacked; and Isabel – flying back in style from Government House in downtown Buenos Aires – was told that the presidential house in the suburb of Olivos, where she thought she was going, was no longer her home. In the official story, she burst into tears, the former cabaret girl who had become the first woman president of Argentina. She was taken first to a city airfield; later she was taken under guard to the presidential house to pack her clothes. There she tried to get the household staff on her side. She thought that they were hers, loyal to her. But they, used to Argentine presidents coming and suddenly going, simply helped her pack.

That was how it ended for her, the poor girl born in the poor northern province of La Rioja. She was in a cabaret in far-off Panama when she met the exiled Perón in 1956, one year after his overthrow, four years after the death of Eva Perón. Isabel was never promoted as a replacement for Eva Perón; and Perón was never reproached by his followers for his association with her. To macho Argentina, infinitely comprehending of a man's needs, Isabel was only the new woman at the leader's side. And when she came back to Argentina with Perón in 1973, she came only as an 'ambassador of peace', the 'verticalizer', the woman who was to bind Argentina with her love, while Perón handled the hate.

'*Perón conduce, Isabel verticaliza*': 'Perón conducts, Isabel verticalizes'. The words are as difficult in Spanish as they are in English; but this was one of the slogans of the last days of Perón's rule, in 1974, when Peronism had already shown itself to be nothing but words, and the rule of Perón and his court was like a continuation of the hysteria that had brought them back; when official printed posters supplemented aerosol graffiti, and the walls of

Buenos Aires were like tattered billboards. So many posters, quickly outdated: always some new martyr to be mourned (and forgotten within a week: nothing as dead, in Peronist Argentina, as last week's political poster), so many killings to be avenged: the leader seeking always to buoy himself up on a collective expression of anger, complaint and hate.

Now there is silence. Isabel is still in detention somewhere in the south, the subject of fading gossip; a private snapshot, released by the authorities, shows that she grew fat during her time in office. Many of the people who ruled with her have scattered. The astrologer López Rega – he was Isabel's manager when she was a cabaret girl in Panama, and he later became Perón's secretary – is out of the country; he has been accused by the present government of embezzling large sums during his time as welfare minister.

The political scandals connected with Perón's return to power, and the financial scandals of his rule and the rule of Isabel, continue. It was the guerrillas who made it possible for Perón to come back; they were the strong right arm of the Peronist movement in 1972 and 1973. But were they all guerrillas? The kidnappings and the bank raids – were they all for the cause? Or was some of the *guerrillerismo* mixed up with Argentine big business? Speculating this time not in land or the falling peso, but in idealism and passion, real blood and torture.

The military like clean walls; and the walls of Buenos Aires are now whitewashed and bare. But here and there the ghostly political graffiti of old times show through the whitewash: the *'Evita Vive'* ('Evita Lives') of 1972; the emblems of the Peronist youth movement; the Peronist election slogan of 1973: *'Cámpora a la Presidencia, Perón al Poder'* ('Cámpora to the Presidency, the Power to Perón'); the later, and Peronistically inevitable, proclamation of *'Cámpora traidor'* ('Cámpora is a traitor'): friend mysteriously turned to enemy, now an unimportant part of dead Argentine history, the ghost of a ghost: all that dead history faint below the military whitewash.

Perón himself is not much talked about now. He is dead; he finally failed everybody; he and the years he wasted can be skipped. History in Argentina is less an attempt to record and understand than a habit of reordering inconvenient facts; it is a process of forgetting. And the middle-class politicians and intellectuals who campaigned for Perón's return, the people who by their unlikely conversion to the Peronist cause made that cause so overwhelming in 1972 and 1973, now avoid the subject or do not come clean.

They say they were hoping to change the movement from within; or they say, more fantastically, that what they really wanted was Peronism without Perón. But it was Perón they invited back from exile to rule over them; and they invited him back – even with his astrologer – because they wanted what he offered.

In her ghosted autobiography, *La Razón de Mi Vida*, Eva Perón say she found out about poverty when she was eleven. 'And the strange thing is that the existence of the poor did not cause me as much pain as the knowledge that at the same time there were people who were rich.' That pain about the rich – that pain about other people – remained the basis of the popular appeal of Peronism. That was the simple passion – rather than 'nationalism' or Perón's 'third position' – that set Argentina alight.

Eva Perón devoted her short political life to mocking the rich, the four hundred families who among them owned most of what was valuable in the million square miles of Argentina. She mocked and wounded them as they had wounded her; and her later unofficial sainthood gave a touch of religion to her destructive cause.

Even when the money ran out, Peronism could offer hate as hope. And in the end that was why Argentina virtually united in calling Perón back, though the first period of his rule had ended in repression and disaster, and though he was very old and close to death. In his eighteen years of exile, while Argentina floundered from government to government, he had remained oddly consistent. He had become the quintessential Argentine: like Eva before him, like all Argentines, he was a victim, someone with enemies, someone with that pain about others. As the years passed, his enemies multiplied; his old words of Argentine complaint began to read like prophecies ('The revolution is without a cause'; 'The military rule but no one obeys'); until finally he appeared to have become the enemy of everybody's enemy.

Peronism was never a programme. It was an insurrection. For more than thirty years Argentina has been in a state of insurrection. The parallel is not with any country in Europe, as Argentine writers sometimes say. The parallel is with Haiti, after the slave rebellion of Toussaint: a barbarous colonial society similarly made, similarly parasitic on a removed civilization, and incapable of regenerating itself because slavery provided the only pattern of human behaviour, and to be a man meant only to be able to assuage that pain about the other, to be like the master.

Eva Perón lit the fire. But the idea of reform was beyond her. She was too wounded, too uneducated; she was too much of her society; and always she was a women among machos. Christophe, emperor of Haiti, built the Citadelle, at immense cost in life as well as money: the model was the British fortifications of Brimstone Hill in the small island of St Kitts, where Christophe was born a slave and trained as a tailor. So Eva Perón in power, obliterating records of her early childhood, yet never going beyond the ideas of childhood, sought only to compete with the rich in their cruelty and wealth and style, their imported goods. It was herself and her triumph that she offered to the people, the *pueblo* in whose name she acted.

Her enemies helped to sanctify her. After Perón's overthrow in 1955 they put on a public display of her clothes, even her intimate garments. She had been dead three years; but that display (especially of the underclothes) was an Argentine, macho form of violation; and the people, *el pueblo*, were meant in addition to be shocked by the extravagance and commonness of their great lady. It was disingenuous: the violators themselves had no higher ideals, and the display of fairy-tale wealth – wealth beyond imagination coming to someone who was of the poor – added to the Evita legend.

Twenty years after her death she found legitimacy. Her small embalmed body – she was five feet two, and at her death she was wasted – now rests at the Duarte family vault in the Recoleta Cemetery, the upper-class necropolis of Buenos Aires. The stone and marble avenues of the mimic town are full of the great names of Argentina, or names which, if the country had been better built, would have been great, but can be seen now only as part of a pretentious, failed past. This legitimacy, this dignity, was all that the girl from Los Toldos wanted; it has taken her an insurrection, an unravelling of the state, to achieve it.

In the early Peronist days she was promoted as a saint, and she is now above Peronism and politics. She is her own cult; she offers protection to those who believe in her. Where there are no reliable institutions or codes or law, no secular assurances, people need faith and magic. And Nature in Argentina is overwhelming: men can feel abandoned in that land of great mountains and big blank spaces. (What desert and scrub and mountains separate the northern province of La Rioja from the softer but still limitless land of the pampa: La Rioja, site of old, lost hope, the town founded in sub-Andean desolation late in the sixteenth century, after Mexico and Peru, as another of the Spanish bases for the search for El Dorado.) Desolation always seems close in the Argentine vastness: how did men come here, how have they endured?

In that desolation cults grow, and they can have a feel of the ancient world. Like the cult of the woman known as *La Difunta Correa*, The Deceased Correa. At some undated time she was crossing the desert on foot. She was starving; there was no water in the desert; and she died. But her baby (or the baby she gave birth to before she died) was found alive, sucking at the breast of the dead woman. Now there are little roadside shrines to her memory, and in these shrines people leave bottles of water. The water evaporates: it has been drunk by the Difunta Correa. *La Difunta Correa tomó el agua:* the simple miracle is ceaselessly renewed.

Eva Perón is that kind of figure now, without dates or politics. And offerings are made at the Duarte vault in the Recoleta. The sarcophagus cannot be seen, but it is known to be there. On the morning I went, white lilies were tied with a white scarf to the black rails, and there was a single faded red rose, unspeakably moving. On the ground, unprotected, was a white mantilla in a plastic wrapper. A woman came with a gift of flowers. She was a woman of the people, with the chunky body of someone whose diet was too starchy. She had come from far, from Mendoza, at the other end of the pampa.

(Mendoza, the wine region at the foot of the Andes, where in the bright southern light and clear air the imported trees of Europe, the willow and the plane, grow gigantically; and the view on one side is always bounded by the grey-blue wall of the mountains. Not the true snow-capped Andes, though: these will appear one day, very far away, apparently unsupported, like a faint white overprinting in the middle sky, giving a new idea of size, awakening wonder not only at the sixteenth-century conquistadores who came this way, but also at the Incas, who, without the wheel, extended their rule so far south, and whose irrigation channels the cultivators of Mendoza still use.)

The lady from Mendoza had a sick daughter – a spastic

or a polio sufferer: it wasn't clear. *'Hace quince años hice la promesa.* I made a vow fifteen years ago.' In 1962, that is, when Eva Perón had been dead for ten years and Perón was still in exile, with no hope of return; when the embalmed body of Eva was presumed lost. Now the miracle had occurred. The body was there; the daughter was well enough again for the vow to be fulfilled.

She placed the flowers on the ground; she went still for a little while, contemplating the rails and the blank vault; and then she became herself again, brisk and ready to go. She said, *'Ya cumplí.* There, I've done it.'

A New King for the Congo:
Mobutu and the Nihilism of Africa

The Congo, which used to be a Belgian colony, is now an African kingdom and is called Zaire. It appears to be a nonsense name, a sixteenth-century Portuguese corruption, some Zairois will tell you, of a local word for 'river'. So it is as if Taiwan, reasserting its Chinese identity, were again to give itself the Portuguese name Formosa. The Congo River is now called the Zaire, as is the local currency, which is almost worthless.

The man who has made himself king of this land of the three Zs – *pays, fleuve, monnaie* – used to be called Joseph Mobutu. His father was a cook. But Joseph Mobutu was educated; he was at some time, in the Belgian days, a journalist. In 1960, when the country became independent, Mobutu was thirty, a sergeant in the local Force Publique. The Force Publique became the Congolese National Army. Mobutu became the colonel and commander, and through the mutinies, rebellions and secessions of the years after independence he retained the loyalty of one paratroop brigade. In 1965, as General Mobutu, he seized power; and as he has imposed order on the army and the country so his style has changed, and become more African. He has abandoned the name of Joseph and is now known as Mobutu Sese Seko Kuku Ngbendu Wa Za Banga.

As General Mobutu he used to be photographed in army uniform. Now, as Mobutu Sese Seko, he wears what he has made, by his example, the Zairois court costume. It is a stylish version of the standard two-piece suit. The jacket has high, wide lapels and is buttoned all the way down; the sleeves can be long or short. A boldly patterned cravat replaces the tie, which has more or less been outlawed; and a breast-pocket handkerchief matches the cravat. On less formal occasions – when he goes among the people – Mobutu wears flowered shirts. Always, in public, he wears a leopard-skin cap and carries an elaborately carved stick.

These – the cap and the stick – are the emblems of his African chieftaincy. Only the chief can kill the leopard. The stick is carved with symbolic figures: two birds, what looks like a snake, a human figure with a distended belly. No Zairois I met could explain the symbolism. One teacher pretended not to know what was carved, and said, 'We would all like to have sticks like that.' In some local carving, though, the belly of the human figure is distended because it contains the fetish. The stick is accepted by Zairois as the stick of the chief. While the chief holds the stick off the ground the people around him can speak; when the chief sets his stick on the ground the people fall silent and the chief gives his decision.

Explaining the constitution and the president's almost unlimited powers, *Profils du Zaire*, the new official handbook (of variable price: four zaires, eight dollars, the pavement seller's 'first' price, two zaires his 'last' price), *Profils du Zaire* quotes Montesquieu on the functions of the state. *Elima*, the official daily, has another, African view of government. 'In Zaire we have inherited from our ancestors a profound respect for the liberties of others. This is why our ancestors were so given to conciliation, people accustomed to the palaver [*la palabre*], accustomed, that is, to discussions that established each man in his rights.'

So Montesquieu and the ancestors are made to meet. And ancestral ways turn out to be advanced. It is only a matter of finding the right words. The palaver is, after all, a 'dialogue'; chief's rule is government by dialogue. But when the chief speaks, when the chief sets his carved stick on the ground, the modern dialogue stops; and Africa of the ancestors takes over. The chief's words, as *Elima* (having it all ways) has sometimes to remind 'anti-revolutionary' elements, cannot be questioned.

It is said that the last five words of Mobutu's African name are a reference to the sexual virility which the African chief must possess: he is the cock that leaves no hen alone. But the words may only be symbolic. Because, as chief, Mobutu is 'married' to his people – 'The Marriage of Sese [Mobutu]' is a 'revolutionary' song – and, as in the good old days of the ancestors, *comme au bon vieux temps de nos ancêtres*, the chief always holds fast to his people. This marriage of the chief can be explained in another, more legalistic way: the chief has a 'contract' with his people. He fulfils his contract through the apparatus of a modern state, but the ministers and commissioners are only the chief's 'collaborators', 'the umbilical cord between the power and the people'.

The chief, the lord wedded to his people, *le pouvoir*: the attributes begin to multiply. Motubu is also the Guide of the Authentic Zairois Revolution, the Father of the Nation, the President-Founder of the Mouvement Populaire de la Révolution, the country's only political party. So that, in nomenclature as in the stylish national dress he has devised, he combines old Africa with what is progressive and new. Just as a Guy Dormeuil suit (160 zaires in the Kinshasa shops, 320 dollars) can, with cravat and matching handkerchief, become an authentic Zairois national costume, so a number of imported glamorous ideas bolster Mobutu's African chieftaincy.

He is citizen, chief, king, revolutionary; he is an African freedom fighter; he is supported by the spirits of the ancestors; like Mao, he has published a book of thoughts (Mobutu's book is green). He has occupied every ideological position and the basis of his kingship cannot be questioned. He rules; he is grand; and, like a medieval king, he is at once loved and feared. He controls the armed forces; they are his creation; in Kinshasa he still sleeps in an army camp. Like Leopold II of the Belgians, in the time of the Congo Free State – much of whose despotic legislation (ownership of the mines in 1888, all vacant lands in 1890, the fruits of the earth in 1891) has passed down through the Belgian colonial administration to the present regime, and is now presented as a kind of ancestral African socialism – like Leopold II, Mobutu owns Zaire.

Muhammad Ali fought George Forman in Kinshasa last November. Ali won; but the victor, in Zaire, was Mobutu. A big hoarding outside the stadium still says, in English below the French: 'A fight between two Blacks [*deux noirs*], in a Black Nation [*un pays de Nègres*] organized by blacks and seen by the whole [world] that is a victory of Mobutism.' And whatever pleasure people had taken in that event, and the publicity, had been dissipated by mid-January, when I arrived. I had chosen a bad time. Mobutu, chieflike, had sprung another of his surprises. A fortnight before, after a two-day palaver with his collaborators, Mobutu had decided on a 'radicalization of the revolution'. And everybody was nervous.

In November 1973 Mobutu had nationalized all businesses and plantations belonging to foreigners – mainly Greeks, Portuguese and Indians – and had given them to Zairois. Now, a year later, he had decided to take back these enterprises, many of them pillaged and bankrupt, and entrust them to the state. What, or who, was the state? No one quite knew. New people, more loyal people? Mobutu, speaking the pure language of revolution, seemed to threaten everybody. The three hundred Belgian families who had ruled the Congo, he said, had been replaced by three hundred Zairois families; the country had imported more Mercedes-Benz motorcars than tractors; one third of the country's foreign earnings went to import food that could be produced at home.

Against this new Zairois bourgeoisie – which he had himself created – the chief now declared war. 'I offer them a clear choice: those among them who love the people should give everything to the state and follow me.' In his new mood the chief threatened other measures. He threatened to close down the cinemas and the nightclubs; he threatened to ban drinking in public places before six.

Through the Belgian-designed *cité indigène* of Kinshasa, in the wide, unpaved streets, full of pits and corrugations between mounds of rubbish sometimes as high as the little houses in Mediterranean colours, in the green shade of flamboyant, mango and frangipani, schoolchildren marched in support of their chief. Every day *Elima* carried reports of *marches de soutien* in other places. And the alarm was great, among the foreigners who had been plundered of their businesses and had remained behind, hoping for some compensation or waiting for Canadian visas, and among the gold-decked Zairois in national costume. Stern men, these Zairois, nervous of the visitor, easily affronted, anxious only to make it known that they were loyal, and outdone by no one in their 'authenticity', their authentic Africanness.

But it is in the nature of a powerful chief that he should be unpredictable. The chief threatens; the people are cowed; the chief relents; the people praise his magnanimity. The days passed; daytime and even morning drinking didn't stop; many Africans continued to spend their days in that red-eyed vacancy that at first so mystifies the visitor. The nightclubs and cinemas didn't close; the prostitutes continued to be busy around the Memling Hotel. So that it seemed that in this matter of public morals, at least, the chief had relented. The ordinary people had been spared.

But the nervousness higher up was justified. Within days the axe fell on many of the chief's 'collaborators'.

There was a shake-up; the circle of power around the chief was made smaller; and Zairois who had ruled in Kinshasa were abruptly dismissed, packed off to unfamiliar parts of the bush to spread the word of the revolution. *Elima* sped them on their way.

The political commissioner will no longer be what he was before the system was modified. That is to say, a citizen floating above the day-to-day realities of the people, driving about the streets and avenues of Kinshasa in a Mercedes and knowing nothing of the life of the peasant of Dumi. The political commissioners will live with the people. They will be in the fields, not as masters but as peasants. They will work with the workers, they will share their joys and sorrows. They will in this way better understand the aspirations of the people and will truly become again children of the people.

Words of terror. Because this was the great fear of so many of the men who had come by riches so easily, by simple official plunder, the new men of the new state who, in the name of Africanization and the dignity of Africa, were so often doing jobs for which they were not qualified and often were drawing salaries for jobs they were not doing at all. This, for all their talk of authenticity and the ways of the ancestors, was their fear: to be returned from the sweet corruptions of Kinshasa to the older corruption of the bush, to be returned to Africa.

And the bush is close. It begins just outside the city and goes on forever. The aeroplane that goes from Kinshasa to Kisangani flies over eight hundred miles of what still looks like virgin forest.

Consider the recent journey of the subregional commissioner of the Equator Region to the settlement of Bomongo. Bomongo lies on the Giri River and is just about one hundred miles north of the big town of

Mbandaka, formerly Coquilhatville, the old 'Equator station', set down more or less on the line of the Equator, halfway on the Congo or Zaire River between Kinshasa and the Stanley Falls. From Mbandaka a steamer took the commissioner's party up the main river to Lubengo; and there they transferred to a dugout for the twenty-mile passage through the Lubengo 'canal' to the Giri River. But the canal for much of its length was only six feet wide, full of snags, and sometimes only twelve inches deep. The outboard motor had to be taken up; paddles had to be used. And there were the mosquitoes.

At the very entrance to the canal [according to the official report in *Elima*], thousands of mosquitoes cover you from head to ankles, compelling you to move about all the time ... After a whole night of insomnia on the Lubengo canal, or rather the 'calvary' of Lubengo, where we had very often to get out in the water and make a superhuman effort to help the paddlers free the pirogue from mud or wood snags, we got to the end of the canal at nine in the morning (we had entered it at 9.30 the previous evening), and so at last we arrived at Bomongo at 12.30, in a state that would have softened the hardest hearts. If we have spoken at some length about the Lubengo canal, it isn't because we want to discourage people from visiting Bomongo by the canal route, but rather to stress one of the main reasons why this place is isolated and seldom visited.

Ignoring his fatigue, *bravant sa fatigue*, the commissioner set to work. He spoke to various groups about the integration of the party and the administration, the need for punctuality, professional thoroughness and revolutionary fervour. The next morning he visited an oil factory in Ebeka district that had been abandoned in 1971 and was now being set going again with the help of a foreign adviser. In the afternoon he spoke out against alcoholism and urged people to produce more. The next day he visited a coffee plantation that had been nationalized in 1973 (the plantations in Zaire were run mainly by Greeks) and given to a Zairois. This particular *attribution* hadn't worked well: the labourers hadn't been paid for the last five months. The labourers complained and the commissioner listened; but what the commissioner did or said wasn't recorded. Everywhere the commissioner went he urged the people, for the sake of their own liberty and well-being, to follow the principles of Mobutism to the letter; everywhere he urged vigilance. Then, leaving Lubengo, Bomongo and Ebeka to the mosquitoes, the commissioner returned to his headquarters. And *Elima* considered the fifteen-day journey heroic enough to give it half a page.

Yet Bomongo, so cut off, is only twenty miles away from the main Congo or Zaire. The roads of the country have decayed; the domestic services of Air Zaire are unreliable; the river remains, in 1975, the great highway of the country. And for nearly a hundred years the river has known steamer traffic. Joseph Conrad, not yet a novelist, going up the river in the wood-burning *Roi des Belges* in 1890, doing eight miles in three hours, halting every night for the cannibal woodcutters to sleep on the riverbank, might have thought he was penetrating to the untouched heart of darkness. But Norman Sherry, the Conrad scholar, has gone among the records and in *Conrad's Western World* has shown that even at the time of Conrad's journey there would have been eleven steamers on the upper river.

The steamers have continued, the Belgian *Otraco* being succeeded by the Zairois *Onatra*. The waterway has been charted: white marker signs are nailed to trees on the banks, the river is regularly cleared of snags. The upstream journey that took one month in Conrad's time now takes seven days; the downstream journey that took a fortnight is now done in five days. The stations have become towns, but they remain what they were: trading outposts. And, in 1975, the journey – one thousand miles between green, flat, almost unchanging country – is still like a journey through nothingness. So little has the vast country been touched: so complete, simple and repetitive still appears the African life through which the traveller swiftly passes.

When the steamer was Belgian, Africans needed a *carte de mérite civique* to travel first class, and third-class African passengers were towed on barges some way behind the steamer. Now the two-tiered third-class barges, rusting, battered, needing paint, full of a busy backyard life, tethered goats and crated chickens packed tight among the passengers, are lashed to the bow of the steamer; and first-class passengers sleep and eat outside their cabin doors in a high, warm smell of smoked fish and smoked monkey.

The *cabine de luxe*, twice as expensive as first class, is used by the sweating *garçon* as a storeroom for his brooms and buckets and rags and as a hiding place for the food, *foo-foo*, he is always on the lookout for: securing half a pound of sugar, for instance, by pouring it into a pot of river-brewed tea, and secreting the tea in the wardrobe until nightfall, when he scratches and bangs and scratches at the door until he is admitted.

The curtains of the *cabine* hang ringless and collapsed. 'C'est pas bon,' the *garçon* says. Many light bulbs are missing; they will now never be replaced; but the empty light brackets on the walls can be used to hang things on. In the bathroom the discased river water looks unfiltered; the stained and leaking wash basin has been pulled out from the wall; the chrome-plated towel rails are forever empty, their function forgotten; and the holes in the floor are mended, like the holes in a dugout, with what looks like mud. The lavatory cistern ceaselessly flushes. 'C'est pas bon,' the *garçon* says, as of an irremediable fact

of life; and he will not say even this when, on an over-
cast afternoon, in a temperature of a hundred degrees,
the windows of the *cabine de luxe* sealed, the air-con-
ditioning unit fails.

The bar is naked except for three bottles of spirits.
Beer is *terminé*, always, though the steamer is full of
dazed Africans and the man known as the maître d'hôtel
is drunk from early morning. There is beer of course;
but every little service requires a 'sweetener'. The
steamer is an African steamer and is run on African
lines. It has been adapted to African needs. It carries
passengers, too many passengers for the two lifeboats
displayed on the first-class deck; but it is more than a
passenger steamer. It is a travelling market; it is, still,
all that many of the people who live along the river
know of the outside world.

The steamer, travelling downstream from Kisangani,
formerly Stanleyville, to Kinshasa, stops only at Bumbe,
Lisala and Mbandaka. But it serves the bush all the
way down. The bush begins just outside Kisangani. The
town ends – the decayed Hôtel des Chutes, the customs
shed, the three or four rusting iron barges moored together, the Roman Catholic cathedral, then a large
ruin, a few riverside villas – and the green begins: bamboo, thick grass spilling over the riverbanks, the earth
showing red, green and red reflected in the smooth water,
the sky, as so often here, dark with storm, lit up and
trembling as with distant gunfire, the light silver. The
wind and rain come; the green bank fades; the water
wrinkles, the reflections go, the water shows muddy.
Jungle seems to be promised. But the bush never grows
high, never becomes forest.

Soon the settlements appear: the low thatched huts
in scraped brown yards, thatch and walls the colour of
the earth, the earth scraped bare for fear of snakes and
soldier ants. Boys swim out to the steamer, their twice-
weekly excitement; and regularly, to shouts, the trading

dugouts come, are skilfully poled in alongside the moving steamer, moored, and taken miles downstream while the goods are unloaded, products of the bush: wicker chairs, mortars carved out of tree trunks, great enamel basins of pineapples. Because of the wars, or for some other reason, there are few men here, and the paddlers and traders are all women, or young girls.

When the traders have sold, they buy. In the forward part of the steamer, beyond the second-class w.c.s, water always running off their steel floors, and in the narrow walk beside the cabins, among the defecating babies, the cooking and the washing and the vacant girls being intently deloused, in a damp smell of salted fish and excrement and oil and rust, and to the sound of gramophone records, there are stalls: razor blades, batteries, pills and capsules, soap, hypodermic syringes, cigarettes, pencils, copybooks, lengths of cloth. These are the products of the outside world that are needed; these are the goods for which such exertions are made. Their business over, the dugouts cast off, to paddle lightless upstream miles in the dark.

There can be accidents (a passenger dugout joining the moving steamer was to be overturned on this journey, and some students returning from the bush to Kinshasa were to be lost); and at night the steamer's searchlights constantly sweep the banks. Moths show white in the light; and on the water the Congo hyacinth shows white: a water plant that appeared on the upper Congo in 1956 and has since spread all the way down, treacherously beautiful, with thick lilylike green leaves and a pale-lilac flower like a wilder hyacinth. It seeds itself rapidly; it can form floating islands that attract other vegetation; it can foul the propellers of the steamer. If the steamers do not fail, if there are no more wars, it is the Congo hyacinth that may yet imprison the river people in the immemorial ways of the bush.

In the morning there are new dugouts, fresh merchandise: basins of slugs in moist black earth, fresh fish, and monkeys, monkeys ready-smoked, *boucané*, charred little hulks, or freshly killed, grey or red monkeys, the tips of their tails slit, the slit skin of the tail tied round the neck, the monkeys bundled up and lifted in this way from the dugouts, by the tails, holdalls, portmanteaux, of dead monkeys. The excitement is great. Monkey is an African delicacy, and a monkey that fetches six zaires, twelve dollars, in Kinshasa can be bought on the river for three zaires.

On the throbbing steel deck the monkeys can appear to be alive and breathing. The wind ruffles their fur; the faces of the red monkeys, falling this way and that, suggest deep contented sleep; their forepaws are loosely closed, sometimes stretched out before them. At the stern of the steamer, on the lower deck, a wood fire is lit and the cooking starts: the dead monkey held face down over the fire, the fur burned off. In the bow, among the goats and hens, there is a wet baby monkey, tightly tethered, somebody's pet or somebody's supper (and in the lifeboat there will appear the next day, as a kind of African joke, a monkey's skull, picked clean and white).

So day after day, through the halts at Bumbe, Lisala and Mbandaka – the two-storeyed Belgian colonial buildings, the ochre concrete walls, the white arches, the green or red corrugated-iron roofs – the steamer market goes on. On the riverbanks bamboo gives way to palms, their lower brown fronds brushing the yellow water. But there is no true forest. The tall trees are dead, and their trunks and bare branches stick out white above the low green bush. The lower vegetation is at times tattered, and sometimes opens out into grassy savanna land, blasted-looking and ghostly in the afternoon heat mist.

The river widens; islands appear; but there is no solitude in this heart of Africa. Always there are the little brown settlements in scraped brown yards, the little plantings of maize or banana or sugar cane about huts, the trading dugouts arriving beside the steamer to shouts.

In the heat mist the sun, an hour before sunset, can appear round and orange, reflected in an orange band in the water muddy with laterite, the orange reflection broken only by the ripples from the bows of the steamer and the barges. Sometimes at sunset the water will turn violet below a violet sky.

But it is a peopled wilderness. The land of this river basin is land used in the African way. It is burned, cultivated, abandoned. It looks desolate, but its riches and fruits are known; it is a wilderness, but one of monkeys. Bush and blasted trees disappear only towards Kinshasa. It is only after nine hundred miles that earth and laterite give way to igneous rocks, and the land, becoming hilly, with sharp indentations, grows smooth and bare, dark with vegetation only in its hollows.

Plant today, reap tomorrow: this is what they say in Kisangani. But this vast green land, which can feed the continent, barely feeds itself. In Kinshasa the meat and even the vegetables have to be imported from other countries. Eggs and orange juice come from South Africa, in spite of hot official words; and powdered milk and bottled milk come from Europe. The bush is a way of life; and where the bush is so overwhelming, organized agriculture is an illogicality.

The Belgians, in the last twenty years of their rule, tried to develop African agriculture, and failed. A girl on the steamer, a teacher, remembered the irrational attempt, and the floggings. Agriculture had to be 'industrialized', a writer said one day in *Elima*, but not in the way 'the old colonialists and their disciples have preached'. The Belgians failed because they were too theoretical, too removed from the peasants, whom they considered 'ignorant' and 'irrational'. In Zaire, as in China, according to this writer, a sound agriculture could only be based on traditional methods. Machines were not necessary. They were not always suited to the soil; tractors, for instance, often made the soil infertile.

Two days later there was another article in *Elima*. It

was no secret, the writer said, that the agriculturists of the country cultivated only small areas and that their production was 'minimal'. Modern machines had to be used: North Korean experts were coming to show the people how. And there was a large photograph of a tractor, a promise of the future.

About agriculture, as about so many things, as about the principles of government itself, there is confusion. Everyone feels the great bush at his back. And the bush remains the bush, with its own logical life. Away from the mining areas and the decaying towns the land is as the Belgians found it and as they have left it.

APERIRE TERRAM GENTIBUS: 'To Open the Land to the Nations': this is the motto, in raised granite, that survives over the defaced monument at Kinshasa railway station. The railway from the Atlantic, the steamer beyond the rapids at Kinshasa: this was how the Congo was opened up, and the monument was erected in 1948 to mark the first fifty years of the railway.

But now the railway is used mainly for goods. Few visitors arrive at the little suburban-style station, still marked 'Kinshasa Est', and step out into the imperial glory of the two-lane boulevard that runs south of the river, just behind the docks. In the roundabout outside the station, the statue of King Albert I, uniformed, with sun helmet and sword (according to old postcards, which continue to be sold), has been taken down; the bronze plaques beside the plinth have been broken away, except for an upper fringe of what looks like banana leaves; the floodlamps have been smashed, the wiring apparatus pulled out and rusted; and all that remains of the monument are two tall brick pillars, like the pillars at the end of some abandoned Congolese Appian Way.

In the station hall the timetable frames swivel empty and glassless on the metal pole. But in the station yard, past the open, unguarded doors, there is a true relic:

an 1893 locomotive, the first used on the Congo railway. It stands on a bed of fresh gravel, amid croton plants and beside two traveller's-trees. It is small, built for a narrow gauge, and looks quaint, with its low, slender boiler, tall funnel and its open cab; but it still appears whole. It is stamped *No. 1* and in an oval cartouche carries one of the great names of the Belgian nineteenth-century industrial expansion: *Société Anonyme John Cockerill – Seraing.*

Not many people in Kinshasa know about this locomotive; and perhaps it has survived because, like so many things of the Belgian past, it is now junk. Like the half-collapsed fork-lift truck on the platform of one of the goods sheds; like the other fork-lift truck in the yard, more thoroughly pillaged, and seemingly decomposed about its rusted forks, which lie in the dust like metal tusks. Like the one-wheel lawn mower in the park outside, which is now a piece of wasteland, overgrown where it has not been scuffed to dust. The lawn mower is in the possession of a little boy, and he, noticing the stranger's interest, rights his machine and skilfully runs it on its one wheel through the dust, making the rusted blades whirr.

The visitor nowadays arrives at the airport of Ndjili, some miles to the east of the city. Zaire is not yet a land for the casual traveller – the harassments, official and unofficial, are too many – and the visitor is usually either a businessman or, if he is black, a delegate (in national costume) to one of the many conferences that Zaire now hosts. From the airport one road leads to the city and the Intercontinental Hotel, past great green-and-yellow boards with Mobutu's sayings in French and English, past the river (the slums of the *cité indigène* well to the south), past the Belgian-built villas in green gardens. A quiet six-lane highway runs twenty or thirty miles in the other direction, to the 'presidential domain' of Nsele.

Here, in what looks like a resort development, flashy

but with hints of perishability, distinguished visitors stay or confer, and good members of the party are admitted to a taste of luxury. Muhammad Ali trained here last year; in January this year some North Korean acrobats and United Nations people were staying. There are air-conditioned bungalows, vast meeting halls, extravagant lounges, a swimming pool. There is also a model farm, run by the Chinese. Nsele is in the style of the new presidency: one of the many grandiloquent official buildings, chief's compounds, that have been set up in the derelict capital in recent years, at once an assertion of the power of the chief and of the primacy of Africa. In the new palace for visiting heads of state the baths are gold-plated: my informant was someone from another African country, who had stayed there.

So the Belgian past recedes and is made to look as shabby as its defaced monuments. *Elima* gives half a page to the fifteen-day journey of the Equator subcommissioner to Bomongo; but Stanley, who pioneered the Congo route, who built the road from Matadi to Kinshasa, has been dethroned. In the museum a great iron wheel from one of the wagons used on that road is preserved by the Belgian curator (and what labour that wheel speaks of); but Mount Stanley is now Mont Ngaliema, a presidential park; and the statue of Stanley that overlooked the rapids has been replaced by the statue of a tall anonymous tribesman with a spear. At the Hôtel des Chutes in Kisangani the town's old name of Stanleyville survives on some pieces of crockery. The broken coffee cups are now used for sugar and powdered milk; when they go the name will have vanished.

The Belgian past is being scrubbed out as the Arab past has been scrubbed out. The Arabs were the Belgians' rivals in the eastern Congo; an Arab was once governor of the Stanley Falls station. But who now associates the Congo with a nineteenth-century Arab empire? A Batetela boy remembered that his ancestors were slave-catchers for the Arabs; they changed sides when the Belgians came and offered them places in their army. But that was long ago. The boy is now a student of psychology, on the lookout, like so many young Zairois, for some foreign scholarship; and the boy's girl friend, of another tribe, people in the past considered enslavable, laughed at this story of slave trading.

The bush grows fast over what were once great events or great disturbances. Bush has buried the towns the Arabs planned, the orchards they planted, as recently, during the post-independence troubles, bush buried the fashionable eastern suburbs of Stanleyville, near the Tshopo falls. The Belgian villas were abandoned; the Africans came first to squat and then to pillage, picking the villas clean of metal, wire, timber, bathtubs and lavatory bowls (both useful for soaking manioc in), leaving only ground-floor shells of brick and masonry. In 1975 some of the ruins still stand, and they look very old, like a tropical, overgrown Pompeii, cleared of its artifacts, with only the ruins of the Château de Venise nightclub giving a clue to the cultural life of the vanished settlement.

And it is surprising how, already, so little of Belgium remains in the minds of people. A man of forty – he had spent some years in the United States – told me that his father, who was born in 1900, remembered the Belgian rubber levy and the cutting off of hands. A woman said that her grandfather had brought white priests to the village to protect the villagers against harsh officials. But, ironically, the people who told these stories both might have been described as *évolués*. Most people under thirty, breaking out of the bush into teaching jobs and administrative jobs in Kinshasa, said they had heard nothing about the Belgians from their parents or grandparents.

One man, a university teacher, said, 'The Belgians gave us a state. Before the Belgians came we had no state.' Another man said he had heard from his grandfather only about the origins of the Bantu people: they wandered south from Lake Chad, crossed the river into an 'empty' country, inhabited only by pygmies, 'a primitive people', whom they drove away into the deep forest. For most the past is a blank; and history begins with their own memories. Most record a village childhood, a school, and then – the shock of independence. To a man from Bandundu, the son of a 'farmer', and the first of his village to be educated, the new world came suddenly in 1960 with the arrival in his village of soldiers of the disintegrating Congolese army. 'I saw soldiers for the first time then, and I was very frightened. They had no officers. They treated the women badly and killed some men. The soldiers were looking for white people.'

In the colonial days, a headmaster told me, the school histories of the Congo began with the late-fifteenth-century Portuguese navigators, and then jumped to the nineteenth century, to the missionaries and the Arabs and the Belgians. African history, as it is now written, restores Africans to Africa, but it is no less opaque: a roll call of tribes, a mention of great kingdoms. So it is in *Introduction à l'Histoire de l'Afrique Noire*, published in Zaire last year. So it is in the official *Profils du Zaire*, which – ignoring Portuguese, missionaries and Arabs – jumps from the brief mention of mostly undated African kingdoms to the establishment of the Congo Free State. The tone is cool and legalistic. King Leopold II's absolute powers are spoken of in just the same way as the powers of older African kings. Passion enters the story only with the events of independence.

The past has vanished. Facts in a book cannot by themselves give people a sense of history. Where so little has changed, where bush and river are so overwhelming, another past is accessible, better answering African bewilderment and African religious beliefs: the past as *le bon vieux temps de nos ancêtres*.

*

In the presidential park at Mont Ngaliema, formerly Mount Stanley, where the guards wear decorative uniforms, and the gates are decorated with bronze plaques – the bad art of modern Africa: art that no longer serves a religious or magical purpose, attempts an alien representationalism and becomes mannered and meaningless, suggesting a double mimicry: African art imitating itself, imitating African-inspired Western art – on Mont Ngaliema there are some colonial graves of the 1890s.

They have been gathered together in neat terraces and are screened by cypress and flamboyant. There, above the rapids – the brown river breaking white on the rocks but oddly static in appearance, the white crests never moving: an eternal level sound of water – the pioneers grandly lie. The simple professions recur: *commis, agent commercial, chaudronnier, capitaine de steamboat, prêtre, s/officier de la Force Publique*. Only Madame Bernard is *sans profession*. Not all were Belgians; some were Norwegians; one missionary was English.

In one kind of imperialist writing these people are heroic. Joseph Conrad, in his passage through the Congo in 1890, just before those burials began on Mont Ngaliema, saw otherwise. He saw people who were too simple for an outpost of progress, people who were part of the crowd at home, and dependent on that crowd, their strength in Africa, like the strength of the Romans in Britain, 'an accident arising from the weakness of others', their 'conquest of the earth' unredeemed by an idea, 'not a sentimental pretence but an idea; and an unselfish belief in the idea'.

'In a hundred years,' Conrad makes one of these simple people say in 'An Outpost of Progress' (1897), 'there will perhaps be a town here. Quays, and warehouses, and barracks, and – and – billiard-rooms. Civilization, my boy, and virtue – and all.' That civilization, so accurately defined, came; and then, like the villas at Stanleyville and the Château de Venise nightclub, vanished. 'Acquisi-

tions, clothes, pretty rags – rags that would fly off at the
first good shake': this is from the narrator of *Heart of
Darkness* (1902). 'No; you want a deliberate belief.'

The people who come now – after the general flight –
are like the people who came then. They offer goods,
deals, technical skills, the same perishable civilization;
they bring nothing else. They are not pioneers; they
know they cannot stay. They fill the nightclubs (now
with African names); they keep the prostitutes (now in
African dress; foreign dress is outlawed for African
women) busy around the Memling Hotel. So, encircled
by Africa, now dangerous again, with threats of expul-
sion and confiscation, outpost civilization continues: at
dinnertime in the Café de la Paix the two old men
parade the young prostitutes they have picked up, girls
of fourteen or fifteen. Old men: their last chance to feed
on such young blood: Kinshasa may close down tomorrow.

'Everyone is here only for the money.' The cynicism
has never been secret; it is now reinforced by anxiety.
With this cynicism, in independent Zaire, the African
can appear to be in complicity. He, too, wants 'acquisi-
tions, clothes, pretty rags': the Mercedes, the fatter prostitutes, the sharp suit with matching handkerchief and
cravat, the gold-rimmed glasses, the gold pen-and-pencil
set, the big gold wristwatch on one hand and the gold
bracelet on the other, the big belly that in a land of
puny men speaks of wealth. But with this complicity and
imitation there is something else: a resentment of the
people imitated, the people now known as *nostalgiques*.

Simon's company, a big one, has been nationalized,
and Simon is now the manager. (Expatriates continue to
do the work, but this is only practical, and Simon doesn't
mind.) Why then does Simon, who has a background of
bush, who is so young and successful, remember his
former manager as a *nostalgique*? Well, one day the
manager was looking through the pay sheets and he said,

'Simon isn't paying enough tax.'

People like Simon (he has an official African name) are not easy to know – even Belgians who speak African languages say that. Simon only answers questions; he is incapable of generating anything like a conversation; because of his dignity, his new sense of the self, the world has closed up for him again; and he appears to be hiding. But his resentment of the former manager must have a deeper cause than the one he has given. And gradually it becomes apparent, from other replies he gives, from his belief in 'authenticity', from his dislike of foreign attitudes to African art (to him a living thing: he considers the Kinshasa museum an absurdity), from the secretive African arrangements of his domestic life (to which he returns in his motorcar), it gradually becomes apparent that Simon is adrift and nervous in this unreal world of imitation.

It is with people like Simon, educated, moneymaking, that the visitor feels himself in the presence of vulnerability, dumbness, danger. Because their resentments, which appear to contradict their ambitions, and which they can never satisfactorily explain, can at any time be converted into a wish to wipe out and undo, an African nihilism, the rage of primitive men coming to themselves and finding that they have been fooled and affronted.

A rebellion like this occurred after independence. It was led by Pierre Mulele, a former minister of education, who, after a long march through the country, camped at Stanleyville and established a reign of terror. Everyone who could read and write had been taken out to the little park and shot; everyone who wore a tie had been shot. These were the stories about Mulele that were circulating in neighbouring Uganda in 1966, nearly two years after the rebellion had been put down (Uganda itself about to crumble, its nihilistic leader already apparent: Amin, the commander of the petty army that

187

had destroyed the Kabaka's power). Nine thousand people are said to have died in Mulele's rebellion. What did Mulele want? What was the purpose of the killings? The forty-year-old African who had spent some time in the United States laughed and said, 'Nobody knows. He was against *everything*. He wanted to start again from the beginning.' There is only one, noncommittal line in *Profils du Zaire* about the Mulelist rebellion. But (unlike Lumumba) he gets a photograph, and it is a big one. It shows a smiling, gap-toothed African – in jacket and tie.

To Joseph Conrad, Stanleyville – in 1890 the Stanley Falls station – was the heart of darkness. It was there, in Conrad's story, that Kurtz reigned, the ivory agent degraded from idealism to savagery, taken back to the earliest ages of man, by wilderness, solitude and power, his house surrounded by impaled human heads. Seventy years later, at this bend in the river, something like Conrad's fantasy came to pass. But the man with 'the inconceivable mystery of a soul that knew no restraint, no faith, and no fear' was black, and not white; and he had been maddened not by contact with wilderness and primitivism, but with the civilization established by those pioneers who now lie on Mont Ngaliema, above the Kinshasa rapids.

Mobutu embodies these African contradictions and, by the grandeur of his kingship, appears to ennoble them. He is, for all his stylishness, the great African nihilist, though his way is not the way of blood. He is the man, 'young but palpitating with wisdom and dynamism' – this is from a University of Zaire publication – who, during the dark days of secessions and rebellions, 'thought through to the heart of the problem' and arrived at his especial illumination: the need for 'authenticity'. 'I no longer have a borrowed conscience. I no longer have a borrowed soul. I no longer speak a borrowed language.' He will bring back ancestral ways and reverences; he will recreate that pure, logical world.

'Our religion is based on a belief in God the creator and the worship of our ancestors.' This is what a minister told teachers the other day. 'Our dead parents are living; it is they who protect us and intercede for us.' No need now for the Christian saints, or Christianity. Christ was the prophet of the Jews and he is dead. Mobutu is the prophet of the Africans. 'This prophet rouses us from our torpor, and has delivered us from our mental alienation. He teaches us to love one another.' In public places the crucifix should be replaced by the image of the messiah, just as in China the portrait of Mao is honoured everywhere. And Mobutu's glorious mother, Mama Yemo, should also be honoured, as the Holy Virgin was honoured.

So Mobutism becomes the African way out. The dances and songs of Africa, so many of them religious in origin, are now officially known as *séances d'animation* and are made to serve the new cult; the dancers wear cloths stamped with Mobutu's image. Old rituals, absorbed into the new, their setting now not the village but the television studio, the palace, the conference hall, appear to have been given fresh dignity. Africa awakes! And, in all things, Mobutu offers himself as the African substitute. At the end of January Mobutu told the Afro-American conference at Kinshasa (sponsored by the Ford and Carnegie foundations): 'Karl Marx is a great thinker whom I respect.' But Marx wasn't always right; he was wrong, for instance, about the beneficial effects of colonialism. 'The teachings of Karl Marx were addressed to his society. The teachings of Mobutu are addressed to the people of Zaire.'

In Africa such comparisons, when they are made, have to be unabashed: African needs are great. And Mobutism is so wrapped up in the glory of Mobutu's kingship – the new palaces (the maharaja-style palace at Kisangani confiscated from Mr Nasser, an old Indian settler), the

189

presidential park at Mont Ngaliema (where Africans walk with foreigners on Sundays and pretend to be amused by the monkeys), the presidential domain at Nsele (open to faithful members of the party: and passengers on the steamer and the barges rush to look), the state visits abroad, intensively photographed, the miracle of the peace Mobutu has brought to the country, the near-absence of policemen in the towns – so glorious are the manifestations of Mobutu's kingship, so good are the words of the king, who proclaims himself a friend of the poor and, as a cook's son, one of the *petit peuple*, that all the contradictions of Africa appear to have been resolved and to have been turned into a kind of power.

But the contradictions remain, and are now sometimes heightened. The newspapers carry articles about science and medicine. But a doctor, who now feels he can say that he cures 'when God and the ancestors wish', tells a newspaper that sterility is either hereditary or caused by a curse; and another newspaper gives publicity to a healer, a man made confident by the revolution, who has an infallible cure for piles, an 'exclusive' secret given him by the ancestors. Agriculture must be modernized, the people must be fed better; but, in the name of authenticity, a doctor warns that babies should on no account be fed on imported foods; traditional foods, like caterpillars and green leaves, are best. The industrialized West is decadent and collapsing; Zaire must rid herself of the plagues of the consumer society, the egoism and individualism exported by industrial civilization. But in the year 2000, according to a university writer in *Elima*, Zaire might herself be booming, with great cities, a population of 'probably' 71,933,851, and a prodigious manufacturing capacity. Western Europe will be in its 'post-industrial' decadence; Russia, Eastern Europe and the Indian subcontinent will form one bloc; Arab oil will be exhausted; and Zaire (and Africa) should have her day, attracting investment from developed countries (obviously those not in decadence), importing factories whole.

So the borrowed ideas – about colonialism and alienation, the consumer society and the decline of the West – are made to serve the African cult of authenticity; and the dream of an ancestral past restored is allied to a dream of a future of magical power. The confusion is not new, and is not peculiar to Zaire. Fantasies like this animated some slave revolts in the West Indies; and today, in Jamaica, at the university, there are people who feel that Negro redemption and Negro power can only come about through a return to African ways. The dead Duvalier of Haiti is admired for his Africanness; a writer speaks, with unconscious irony, of the Negro's need for a 'purifying' period of poverty (unwittingly echoing Duvalier's 'It is the destiny of the people of Haiti to suffer'); and there are people who, sufficiently far away from the slaughter ground of Uganda, find in Amin's African nihilism a proof of African power.

It is lunacy, despair. In the February 7th issue of *Jeune Afrique* – miraculously on sale in Kinshasa – a French African writer, Seydou Lamine, examines the contradictions of African fantasy and speaks of 'the alibi of the past'. Mightn't this talk of Africanness, he asks, be a 'myth' which the 'princes' of Africa now use to strengthen their own position? 'For many, authenticity and Negroness [*la négrité*] are only words that stand for the despair and powerlessness of the man of Africa faced with the discouraging immensity of his underdevelopment.'

And even *Elima*, considering the general corruption, the jobs not done, the breakdown of municipal administration in Kinshasa, the uncleared garbage, the canals not disinfected (though the taxis are, regularly, for the one-zaire fee), the vandalized public television sets and telephone booths, even *Elima* finds it hard on some days to blame the colonial past for these signs of egoism. 'We are wrong to consider the word "underdevelopment" only in its economic aspects. We have to understand that there is a type of underdevelopment that issues out of the habits of a people and their attitudes to life and society.'

Mobutism, *Elima* suggests, will combat this 'mental plague'. But it is no secret that, in spite of its talk of 'man', in spite of its lilting national anthem called the *Zairoise* ('*Paix, justice et travail*'), Mobutism honours only one man: the chief, the king. He alone has to be feared and loved. How – away from this worship – does a new attitude to life and society begin? Recently in Kinshasa a number of people were arrested for some reason and taken to Makala gaol: lavatoryless concrete blocks behind a whitewashed wall, marked near the gateway DISCIPLINE AVANT TOUT. The people arrested couldn't fit easily into the cell, and a Land-Rover was used to close the door. In the morning many were found crushed or suffocated.

Not cruelty, just thoughtlessness: the visitor has to learn to accommodate himself to Zaire. The presidential domain at Nsele (where Muhammad Ali trained) is such a waste, at once extravagant and shoddy, with its over-furnished air-conditioned bungalows, its vast meeting halls, its VIP lounges (carpets, a fussiness of fringed Dralon, African art debased to furniture decoration). But Nsele can be looked at in another way. It speaks of the African need for African style and luxury; it speaks of the great African wound. The wound explains the harassment of foreign settlers, the nationalizations. But the nationalizations are petty and bogus; they have often turned out to be a form of pillage and are part of no creative plan; they are as short-sighted, self-wounding and nihilistic as they appear, a dismantling of what remains of the Belgian-created state. So the visitor swings from mood to mood, and one reaction cancels out another.

Where, in Kinshasa, where so many people 'shadow'

jobs. and so many jobs are artificial and political, part of an artificial administration, where does the sense of responsibility, society, the state, begin? A city of two million, with almost no transport, with no industries (save for those assembly plants, sited, as in so many 'developing' countries, on the road from the airport to the capital), a city detached from the rest of the country, existing only because the Belgians built it and today almost without a point. It doesn't have to work; it can be allowed to look after itself. Already at night, a more enduring kind of bush life seems to return to central Kinshasa, when the watchmen (who also shadow their jobs: they will protect nothing) bar off their territory, using whatever industrial junk there is to hand, light fires on the broken pavements, cook their little messes and go to sleep. When it is hot the gutters smell; in the rain the streets are flooded. And the unregulated city spreads: meandering black rivulets of filth in unpaved alleys, middens beside the highways, children, discarded motorcar tyres, a multitude of little stalls, and everywhere, in free spaces, plantings of sugar cane and ...aize: subsistence agriculture in the town, a remnant of bush life.

But at the end of one highway there is the university. It is said to have gone down. But the students are bright and friendly. They have come from the bush, but already they can talk of Stendhal and Fanon; they have the enthusiasm of people to whom everything is new; and they feel, too, that with the economic collapse of the West (of which the newspapers talk every day) the tide is running Africa's way. The enthusiasm deserves a better-equipped country. It seems possible that many of these students, awakening to ideas, history, a knowledge of injustice and a sense of their own dignity, will find themselves unsupported by their society, and can only awaken to pain. But no. For most there will be jobs in the government; and already they are Mobutists to a man.

Already the African way ahead is known; already inquiry is restricted; and Mobutu himself has warned that the most alienated people in Zaire are the intellectuals.

So Mobutism simplifies the world, the concept of responsibility and the state, and simplifies people. Zaire's accession to power and glory has been made to appear so easy; the plundering of the inherited Belgian state has been so easy, the confiscations and nationalizations, the distribution of big shadow jobs. Creativity itself now begins to appear as something that might be looted, brought into being by decree.

Zaire has her music and dance. To complete her glory, Zaire needs a literature; other African countries have literatures. The trouble, *Elima* says in a full-page Sunday article, is that far too many people who haven't written a line and sometimes can't even speak correctly have been going here and there and passing themselves off as Zairois writers, shaming the country. That will now stop; the bogus literary 'circles' will be replaced by official literary 'salons'; and they must set to work right away. In two months the president will be going to Paris. The whole world will be watching, and it is important that in these two months a work of Zairois literature be written and published. Other works should be produced for the Lagos Festival of Negro Arts at the end of the year. And it seems likely, from the tone of the *Elima* article, that it is Mobutu who has spoken.

Mobutu speaks all the time. He no longer speaks in French but in Lingala, the local lingua franca, and transistors take his words to the deep bush. He speaks as the chief, and the people listen. They laugh constantly, and they applaud. It has been Mobutu's brilliant idea to give the people of Zaire what they have not had and what they have long needed: an African king. The king expresses all the dignity of his people; to possess a king is to share the king's dignity. The individual's responsibility – a possible source of despair, in the abjectness of Africa – is lessened. All that is required is obedience, and obedience is easy.

Mobutu proclaims his simple origins. He is a *citoyen* like everyone else. And Mama Mobutu, Mobutu's wife, loves the poor. She runs a centre for deprived girls, and they devote themselves to agriculture and to making medallions of the king, which the loyal will wear: there can never be too many images of Mobutu in Zaire. The king's little magnanimities are cherished by a people little used to magnanimity. Many Zairois will tell you that a hospital steamer now serves the river villages. But it is where Mobutu appears to be most extravagant that he satisfies his people most. The king's mother is to be honoured; and she was a simple woman of Africa. Pilgrimages are announced to places connected with the king's life; and the disregarded bush of Africa becomes sacred again.

The newspapers, diluting the language of Fanon and Mao, speak every day of the revolution and the radicalization of the revolution. But this is what the revolution is about: the kingship. In Zaire Mobutu is the news: his speeches, his receptions, the *marches de soutien*, the new appointments: court news. Actual events are small. The nationalization of a gaudy furniture shop in Kinshasa is big news, as is the revelation that there is no African on the board of a brewery. Anti-revolutionary activity, discovered by the 'vigilance' of the people, has to do with crooked vendors in the market, an official using a government vehicle as a night taxi, someone else building a house where he shouldn't, some drunken members of the youth wing of the party wrecking the party Volkswagen at Kisangani. There is no news in Zaire because there is little new activity. Copper continues to be mined; the big dam at Inga continues to be built. Airports are being extended or constructed everywhere, but this doesn't mean that Air Zaire is booming:

it is for the better policing of the country.

What looked obvious on the first day, but was then blurred by the reasonable-sounding words, turns out to be true. The kingship of Mobutu has become its own end. The inherited modern state is being dismantled, but it isn't important that the state should work. The bush works; the bush has always been self-sufficient. The administration, now the court, is something imposed, something unconnected with the true life of the country. The ideas of responsibility, the state and creativity are ideas brought by the visitor; they do not correspond, for all the mimicry of language, to African aspirations.

Mobutu's peace and his kingship are great achievements. But the kingship is sterile. The cult of the king already swamps the intellectual advance of a people who have barely emerged. The intellectual confusions of authenticity, that now give such an illusion of power, close up the world again and point to a future greater despair. Mobutu's power will inevitably be extinguished; but there can now be no going back on the principles of Mobutism. Mobutu has established the pattern for his successors; and they will find that African dependence is not less than it is now, nor the need for nihilistic assertion.

To arrive at this sense of a country trapped and static, eternally vulnerable, is to begin to have something of the African sense of the void. It is to begin to fall, in the African way, into a dream of a past – the vacancy of river and forest, the hut in the brown yard, the dugout – when the dead ancestors watched and protected, and the enemies were only men.

Conrad's Darkness

It has taken me a long time to come round to Conrad. And if I begin with an account of his difficulty, it is because I have to be true to my experience of him. I would find it hard to be detached about Conrad. He was, I suppose, the first modern writer I was introduced to. It was through my father. My father was a self-taught man, picking his way through a cultural confusion of which he was perhaps hardly aware and which I have only recently begun to understand; and he wished himself to be a writer. He read less for pleasure than for clues, hints and encouragement; and he introduced me to those writers he had come upon in his own search. Conrad was one of the earliest of these: Conrad the stylist, but more than that, Conrad the late starter, holding out hope to those who didn't seem to be starting at all.

I believe I was ten when Conrad was first read to me. It sounds alarming; but the story was 'The Lagoon'; and the reading was a success. 'The Lagoon' is perhaps the only story of Conrad's that can be read to a child. It is very short about fifteen pages. A forest-lined tropical river at dusk. The white man in the boat says, 'We'll spend the night in Arsat's clearing.' The boat swings into a creek; the creek opens out into a lagoon. A lonely house on the shore; inside, a woman is dying. And during the night Arsat, the young man who is her lover, will tell how they both came there. It is a story of illicit love in another place, an abduction, a chase, the death of a brother, abandoned to the pursuers. What Arsat has to say should take no more than fifteen minutes; but romance is romance, and when Arsat's story ends the dawn comes up; the early-morning breeze blows away the mist; the woman is dead. Arsat's happiness, if it existed, has been flawed and brief; and now he will leave the lagoon and go back to his own place, to meet his fate. The white man, too, has to go. And the last picture is of Arsat, alone in his lagoon, looking 'beyond the great light of a cloudless day into the darkness of a world of illusions'.

In time the story of 'The Lagoon' became blurred. But the sense of night and solitude and doom stayed with me, grafted, in my fantasy, to the South Sea or tropical island setting of the Sabu and Jon Hall films. I have, unwillingly, looked at 'The Lagoon' again. There is a lot of Conrad in it – passion and the abyss, solitude and futility and the world of illusions – and I am not sure now that it isn't the purest piece of fiction Conrad wrote. The brisk narrative, the precise pictorial writing, the setting of river and hidden lagoon, the nameless white visitor, the story during the night of love and loss, the death at daybreak: everything comes beautifully together. And if I say it is a pure piece of fiction, it is because the story speaks for itself; the writer does not come between his story and the reader.

'The Lagoon' was parodied by Max Beerbohm in 'A Christmas Garland'. Writers' myths can depend on accidents like that. 'The Lagoon', as it happens, was the first short story Conrad wrote; and though later, when I read the parody, I was able to feel that I was in the know about Conrad, from my own point of view 'The Lagoon' had been a cheat. Because I was never to find anything so strong and direct in Conrad again.

There is a story, 'Karain', written not long after 'The Lagoon'. It has the same Malayan setting and, as Conrad acknowledged, a similar motif. Karain, inspired by sudden sexual jealousy, kills the friend whose love quest he had promised to serve; and thereafter Karain is haunted by the ghost of the man he has killed. One day he meets a wise old man, to whom he confesses. The old man exorcises the ghost; and Karain, with the old man as his counsellor, becomes a warrior and a conqueror, a ruler. The old man dies; the ghost of the murdered friend returns to haunt Karain. He is immediately lost; his power and splendour are nothing; he swims out to the white men's ship and asks them, unbelievers from another world, for help. They give him a charm: a Jubilee sixpence. The charm works; Karain becomes a man again.

The story is, on the surface, a yarn about native superstition. But to Conrad it is much more; it is profounder, and more wonderful, than 'The Lagoon'; and he is determined that its whole meaning should be grasped. All the suggestions that were implicit in 'The Lagoon' are now spelled out. The white men have names; they talk, and act as a kind of chorus. So we are asked to contemplate the juxtaposition of two cultures, one open and without belief, one closed and ruled by old magic; one, 'on the edge of outer darkness', exploring the world, one imprisoned in a small part of it. But illusions are illusions, mirage is mirage. Isn't London itself, the life of its streets, a mirage? 'I see it. It is there; it pants, it runs; it rolls; it is strong and alive; it would smash you if you didn't look out; but I'll be hanged if it is yet as real to me as the other thing.' So, romantically and somewhat puzzlingly, the story ends.

The simple yarn is made to carry a lot. It requires a more complex response than the plainer fiction of 'The Lagoon'. Sensations – night and solitude and doom – are not enough; the writer wishes to involve us in more than his fantasy; we are required – the chorus or commentary requires us – to stand outside the facts of the story and contemplate the matter. The story has become a kind of parable. Nothing has been rigged, though, because nothing is being proved; only wonder is being awakened.

In a preface to a later collection of stories Conrad wrote: 'The romantic feeling of reality was in me an inborn faculty.' He hadn't deliberately sought out romantic subjects; they had offered themselves to him.

> I have a natural right to [my subjects] because my past is very much my own. If their course lies out of the beaten path of organized social life, it is, perhaps, because I myself did in a sort break away from it early in obedience to an impulse which must have been very genuine since it has sustained me through all the dangers of disillusion. But that origin of my literary work was very far from giving a larger scope to my imagination. On the contrary, the mere fact of dealing with matters outside the general run of every day experience laid me under the obligation of a more scrupulous fidelity to the truth of my own sensations. The problem was to make unfamiliar things credible. To do that I had to create for them, to reproduce for them, to envelop them in their proper atmosphere of actuality. This was the hardest task of all and the most important, in view of that conscientious rendering of truth in thought and fact which has been always my aim.

But the truths of that story, 'Karain', are difficult ones. The world of illusions, men as prisoners of their cultures, belief and unbelief: these are truths one has to be ready for, and perhaps half possess already, because the story does not carry them convincingly within itself. The suggestion that the life of London is as much a mirage as the timeless life of the Malayan archipelago is puzzling, because the two-page description of the London streets with which the story ends is too literal: blank faces, hansom cabs, omnibuses, girls 'talking vivaciously', 'dirty men ... discussing filthily', a policeman. There isn't anything in that catalogue that can persuade us that the life described is a mirage. Reality hasn't fused with the writer's fantasy. The concept of the mirage has to be applied. it is a matter of words, a disturbing caption to a fairly straight picture.

I have considered this simple story at some length because it illustrates, in little, the difficulties I was to have with the major works. I felt with Conrad I wasn't getting the point. Stories, simple in themselves, always seemed at some stage to elude me. And there were the words, the words that issued out of the writer's need to be faithful to the truth of his own sensations. The words got in the way; they obscured. *The Nigger of the Narcissus* and *Typhoon*, famous books, were impenetrable.

In 1896 the young H. G. Wells, in an otherwise kind review of *An Outcast of the Islands*, the book before *The Nigger*, wrote: 'Mr Conrad is wordy; his story is not so much told as seen intermittently through a haze of sentences. He has still to learn the great half of his art, the art of leaving things unwritten.' Conrad wrote a friendly letter to Wells; but on the same day – the story is in Jocelyn Baines's biography – he wrote to Edward Garnett: 'Something brings the impression off – makes its effect. What? It can be nothing but the expression – the arrangement of words, the style.' It is, for a novelist, an astonishing definition of style. Because style in the novel, and perhaps in all prose, is more than an 'arrangement of words': it is an arrangement, even an orchestration, of perceptions, it is a matter of knowing where to put what. But Conrad aimed at fidelity. Fidelity required him to be explicit.

It is this explicitness, this unwillingness to let the story speak for itself, this anxiety to draw all the mystery out of a straightforward situation, that leads to the mystification of *Lord Jim*. It isn't always easy to know what is being explained. The story is usually held to be about honour. I feel myself that it is about the theme – much more delicate in 1900 than today – of the racial straggler. And, such is Conrad's explicitness, both points of view can be supported by quotation. *Lord Jim*, however, is an imperialist book, and it may be that the two points of view are really one.

Whatever the mystery of *Lord Jim*, it wasn't of the sort that could hold me. Fantasy, imagination, story if you like, had been refined away by explicitness. There was something unbalanced, even unfinished, about Conrad. He didn't seem able to go beyond his first simple conception of a story; his invention seemed to fail so quickly. And even in his variety there was something tentative and uncertain.

There was *The Secret Agent*, a police thriller that seemed to end almost as soon as it began, with a touch of Arnold Bennett and *Riceyman Steps* in that Soho interior, and a Wellsian jokeyness about London street names and cabbies and broken-down horses – as though, when dealing with the known, the written about, the gift of wonder left the writer and he had to depend on other writers' visions. There was *Under Western Eyes*, which, with its cast of Russian revolutionaries and its theme of betrayal, promised to be Dostoevskyan but then dissolved away into analysis. There was the too set-up fiction of *Victory*: the pure, aloof man rescues a girl from a musical company touring the East and takes her to a remote island, where disaster, in the form of gangsters, will come to them. And there was *Nostromo*, about South America, a confusion of characters and themes, which I couldn't get through at all.

A multiplicity of Conrads, and they all seemed to me to be flawed. The hero of *Victory*, holding himself aloof from the world, had 'refined away everything except disgust'; and it seemed to me that in his fictions Conrad had refined away, as commonplace, those qualities of imagination and fantasy and invention that I went to novels for. The Conrad novel was like a simple film with an elaborate commentary. A film: the characters and settings could be seen very clearly. But realism often required trivial incidental dialogue, the following of trivial actions; the melodramatic flurry at the end emphasized the slowness and bad proportions of what had gone before; and the commentary emphasized the fact that the characters were actors.

But we read at different times for different things. We take to novels our own ideas of what the novel should be; and those ideas are made by our needs, our education, our background or perhaps our ideas of our background. Because we read, really, to find out what we already know, we can take a writer's virtues for granted. And his originality, the news he is offering us, can go over our heads.

It came to me that the great novelists wrote about highly organized societies. I had no such society; I couldn't share the assumptions of the writers; I didn't see my world reflected in theirs. My colonial world was more mixed and secondhand, and more restricted. The time came when I began to ponder the mystery – Conradian word – of my own background: that island in the mouth of a great South American river, the Orinoco, one of the Conradian dark places of the earth, where my father had conceived literary ambitions for himself and then for me, but from which, in my mind, I had stripped all romance and perhaps even reality: preferring to set 'The Lagoon', when it was read to me, not on the island I knew, with its muddy rivers, mangrove and swamps, but somewhere far away.

It seemed to me that those of us who were born there were curiously naked, that we lived purely physically. It wasn't an easy thing to explain, even to oneself. But in Conrad, in that very story of 'Karain', I was later to find my feelings about the land exactly caught.

And really, looking at that place, landlocked from the sea and shut off from the land by the precipitous slopes of mountains, it was difficult to believe in the existence of any neighbourhood. It was still, complete, unknown, and full of a life that went on stealthily with a troubling effect of solitude; of a life that seemed unaccountably empty of anything that would stir the thought, touch the heart, give a hint of the ominous sequence of days. It appeared to us a land without memories, regrets, and hopes; a land where nothing could survive the coming of the night, and where each sunrise, like a dazzling act of special creation, was disconnected from the eve and the morrow.

It is a passage that, earlier, I would have hurried through: the purple passage, the reflective caption. Now I see a precision in its romanticism, and a great effort of thought and sympathy. And the effort doesn't stop with the aspect of the land. It extends to all men in these dark or remote places who, for whatever reason, are denied a clear vision of the world: Karain himself, in his world of phantoms; Wang, the self-exiled Chinese of *Victory*, self-contained within the 'instinctive existence' of the Chinese peasant; the two Belgian empire builders of 'An Outpost of Progress', helpless away from their fellows, living in the middle of Africa 'like blind men in a large room, aware only of what came in contact with them, but unable to see the general aspect of things'.

'An Outpost of Progress' is now to me the finest thing Conrad wrote. It is the story of two commonplace Belgians, new to the new Belgian Congo, who find that they have unwittingly, through their Negro assistant, traded Africans for ivory, are then abandoned by the surrounding tribesmen, and go mad. But my first judgement of it had been only literary. It had seemed familiar; I had read other stories of lonely white men going mad in hot countries. And my rediscovery, or discovery, of Conrad really began with one small scene in *Heart of Darkness*.

The African background – 'the demoralized land' of

plunder and licensed cruelty – I took for granted. That is how we can be imprisoned by our assumptions. The background now seems to me to be the most effective part of the book; but then it was no more than what I expected. The story of Kurtz, the upriver ivory agent, who is led to primitivism and lunacy by his unlimited power over primitive men, was lost on me. But there was a page which spoke directly to me, and not only of Africa.

The steamer is going upriver to meet Kurtz; it is 'like travelling back to the earliest beginnings of the world'. A hut is sighted on the bank. It is empty, but it contains one book, sixty years old, *An Inquiry into Some Points of Seamanship*, tattered, without covers, but 'lovingly stitched afresh with white cotton thread'. And in the midst of nightmare, this old book, 'dreary ... with illustrative diagrams and repulsive tables of figures', but with its 'singleness of intention', its 'honest concern for the right way of going to work', seems to the narrator to be 'luminous with another than a professional light'.

This scene, perhaps because I have carried it for so long, or perhaps because I am more receptive to the rest of the story, now makes less of an impression. But I suppose that at the time it answered something of the political panic I was beginning to feel.

To be a colonial was to know a kind of security; it was to inhabit a fixed world. And I suppose that in my fantasy I had seen myself coming to England as to some purely literary region, where, untrammelled by the accidents of history or background, I could make a romantic career for myself as a writer. But in the new world I felt that ground move below me. The new politics, the curious reliance of men on institutions they were yet working to undermine, the simplicity of beliefs and the hideous simplicity of actions, the corruption of causes, half-made societies that seemed doomed to remain half-made: these were the things that began to preoccupy me. They were not things from which I could detach myself. And I found that Conrad – sixty years before, in the time of a great peace – had been everywhere before me. Not as a man with a cause, but a man offering, as in *Nostromo*, a vision of the world's half-made societies as places which continuously made and unmade themselves, where there was no goal, and where always 'something inherent in the necessities of successful action ... carried with it the moral degradation of the idea'. Dismal, but deeply felt: a kind of truth and half a consolation.

To understand Conrad, then, it was necessary to begin to match his experience. It was also necessary to lose one's preconceptions of what the novel should do and, above all, to rid oneself of the subtle corruptions of the novel or comedy of manners. When art copies life, and life in its turn mimics art, a writer's originality can often be obscured. *The Secret Agent* seemed to be a thriller. But Inspector Heat, correct but oddly disturbing, was like no policeman before in fiction – though there have been many like him since. And, in spite of appearances, this grand lady, patroness of a celebrated anarchist, was not Lady Bracknell:

> His views had nothing in them to shock or startle her, since she judged them from the standpoint of her lofty position. Indeed, her sympathies were easily accessible to a man of that sort. She was not an exploiting capitalist herself; she was, as it were, above the play of economic conditions. And she had a great pity for the more obvious forms of common human miseries, precisely because she was such a complete stranger to them that she had to translate her conception into terms of mental suffering before she could grasp the notion of their cruelty ... She had come to believe almost his theory of the future, since it was not repugnant to her prejudices. She disliked the new element of plutocracy in the social compound, and industrialism as a method of human development

appeared to her singularly repulsive in its mechanical and unfeeling character. The humanitarian hopes of the mild Michaelis tended not towards utter destruction, but merely towards the economic ruin of the system. And she did not really see where was the moral harm of it. It would do away with all the multitude of the parvenus, whom she disliked and mistrusted, not because they had arrived anywhere (she denied that), but because of their profound unintelligence of the world, which was the primary cause of the crudity of their perceptions and the aridity of their hearts.

Not Lady Bracknell. Someone much more real, and still recognizable in more than one country. Younger today perhaps; but humanitarian concern still disguises a similar arrogance and simplicity, the conviction that wealth, a particular fortune, position or a particular name are the only possible causes of human self-esteem. And in how many countries today can we find the likeness of this man?

The all but moribund veteran of dynamite wars had been a great actor in his time ... The famous terrorist had never in his life raised personally so much as his little finger against the social edifice. He was no man of action ... With a more subtle intention, he took the part of an insolent and venomous evoker of sinister impulses which lurk in the blind envy and exasperated vanity of ignorance, in the suffering and misery of poverty, in all the hopeful and noble illusions of righteous anger, pity and revolt. The shadow of his evil gift clung to him yet like the smell of a deadly drug in an old vial of poison, emptied now, useless, ready to be thrown away upon the rubbish-heap of things that had served their time.

The phrase that had struck me there was 'sinister impulses which lurk in ... noble illusions'. But now another phrase stands out: the 'exasperated vanity of ignorance'.

It is so with the best of Conrad. Words which at one time we disregard, at another moment glitter.

But the character in *The Secret Agent* who is the subject of that paragraph hardly exists outside that paragraph. His name is Karl Yundt; he is not one of the figures we remember. Physically, he is a grotesque, a caricature, as are so many of the others, for all Conrad's penetration – anarchists, policemen, government ministers. There is nothing in Karl Yundt's dramatic appearance in the novel, so to speak, that matches the profundity of that paragraph or hints at the quality of reflection out of which he was created.

My reservations about Conrad as a novelist remain. There is something flawed and unexercised about his creative imagination. He does not – except in *Nostromo* and some of the stories – involve me in his fantasy; and *Lord Jim* is still to me more acceptable as a narrative poem than as a novel. Conrad's value to me is that he is someone who sixty to seventy years ago meditated on my world, a world I recognize today. I feel this about no other writer of the century. His achievement derives from the honesty which is part of his difficulty, that 'scrupulous fidelity to the truth of my own sensations'.

Nothing is rigged in Conrad. He doesn't remake countries. He chose, as we now know, incidents from real life; and he meditated on them. 'Meditate' is his own, exact word. And what he says about his heroine in *Nostromo* can be applied to himself. 'The wisdom of the heart having no concern with the erection or demolition of theories any more than with the defence of prejudices, has no random words at its command. The words it pronounces have the value of acts of integrity, tolerance and compassion.'

Every great writer is produced by a series of special circumstances. With Conrad these circumstances are well known: his Polish youth, his twenty years of wandering, his settling down to write in his late thirties, experience more or less closed, in England, a foreign country. These circumstances have to be considered together; one cannot be stressed above any other. The fact of the late start cannot be separated from the background and the scattered experience. But the late start is important.

Most imaginative writers discover themselves, and their world, through their work. Conrad, when he settled down to write, was, as he wrote to the publisher William Blackwood, a man whose character had been formed. He knew his world, and had reflected on his experience. Solitariness, passion, the abyss: the themes are constant in Conrad. There is a unity in a writer's work; but the Conrad who wrote *Victory*, though easier and more direct in style, was no more experienced and wise than the Conrad who, twenty years before, had written *Almayer's Folly*. His uncertainties in the early days seem to have been mainly literary, a trying out of subjects and moods. In 1896, the year after the publication of *Almayer's Folly*, he could break off from the romantic turgidities of *The Rescue* and write not only 'The Lagoon', but also begin 'An Outpost of Progress'. These stories, which stand at the opposite ends, as it were, of my comprehension of Conrad, one story so romantic, one so brisk and tough, were written almost at the same time.

And there are the aphorisms. They run right through Conrad's work, and their tone never varies. It is the same wise man who seems to be speaking. 'The fear of finality which lurks in every human breast and prevents so many heroisms and so many crimes': that is from *Almayer's Folly*, 1895. And this is from *Nostromo*, 1904: 'a man to whom love comes late, not as the most splendid of illusions, but like an enlightening and priceless misfortune' – which is almost too startling in the context. From *The Secret Agent*, 1907, where it seems almost wasted: 'Curiosity being one of the forms of self-revelation, a systematically incurious person remains always partly mysterious.' And lastly, from *Victory*, 1915: 'the fatal imperfection of all the gifts of life, which makes of them a delusion and a snare' – which might have been fitted into any of the earlier books.

To take an interest in a writer's work is, for me, to take an interest in his life; one interest follows automatically on the other. And to me there is something peculiarly depressing about Conrad's writing life. With a writer like Ibsen one can be as unsettled by the life as by the plays themselves. One wonders about the surrender of the life of the senses; one wonders about the short-lived satisfactions of the creative instinct, as unappeasable as the senses. But with Ibsen there is always the excitement of the work, developing, changing, enriched by these very doubts and conflicts. All Conrad's subjects, and all his conclusions, seem to have existed in his head when he settled down to write. *Nostromo* could be suggested by few lines in a book, *The Secret Agent* by a scrap of conversation and a book. But, really, experience was in the past; and the labour of the writing life lay in dredging up this experience, in 'casting round' – Conradian words – for suitable subjects for meditation.

Conrad's ideas about fiction seem to have shaped early during his writing career. And, whatever the uncertainties of his early practice, these ideas never changed. In 1895, when his first book was published, he wrote to a friend, who was also beginning to write: 'All the charm, all the truth of [your story] are thrown away by the construction – by the mechanism (so to speak) of the story which makes it appear false ... You have much imagination: much more than I ever will have if I live to be a hundred years old. Well, that imagination (I wish I had it) should be used to create human souls: to disclose human hearts – and not to create events that are properly speaking *accidents* only. To accomplish it you must cultivate your poetic faculty ... you must squeeze out of yourself every sensation, every thought, every image.' When he met Wells, Conrad said (the story is Wells's): 'My dear Wells, what is this *Love and Mr Lewisham* about? What is all this about Jane Austen? What is it all *about*?' And later – all these quotations are from Jocelyn Baines's biography – Conrad was to write: 'The national English novelist seldom regards his work – the exercise of his Art – as an achievement of active life by which he will produce certain definite effects upon the emotions of his readers, but simply as an instinctive, often unreasoned, outpouring of his own emotions.'

Were these ideas of Conrad's French and European? Conrad, after all, liked Balzac, most breathless of writers; and Balzac, through instinct and unreason, a man bewitched by his own society, had arrived at something very like that 'romantic feeling of reality' which Conrad said was his own inborn faculty. It seems at least possible that, in his irritated rejection of the English novel of manners and the novel of 'accidents', Conrad was rationalizing what was at once his own imaginative deficiency as well as his philosophical need to stick as close as possible to the facts of every situation. In fiction he did not seek to discover; he sought only to explain; the discovery of every tale, as the narrator of *Under Western Eyes* says, is a moral one.

In the experience of most writers the imaginative realizing of a story constantly modifies the writer's original concept of it. Out of experience, fantasy and all kinds of impulses, a story suggests itself. But the story has to be tested by, and its various parts survive, the writer's dramatic imagination. Things work or they don't work; what is true feels true; what is false is false. And the writer, trying to make his fiction work, making accommodations with his imagination, can say more than he knows. With Conrad the story seems to be fixed; it is something given, like the prose 'argument' stated at the beginning of a section of an old poem. Conrad knows exactly what he has to say. And sometimes, as in *Lord Jim* and *Heart of Darkness*, he says less than he intends.

Heart of Darkness breaks into two. There is the reportage about the Congo, totally accurate, as we now know: Conrad scholarship has been able to identify almost everyone in that story. And there is the fiction, which in the context is like fiction, about Kurtz, the ivory agent who allows himself to become a kind of savage African god. The idea of Kurtz, when it is stated, seems good: he will show 'what particular region of the first ages a man's untrammelled feet may take him into by way of solitude'. Beguiling words, but they are abstract; and the idea, deliberately worked out, remains an applied idea. Conrad's attitude to fiction – not as something of itself, but as a varnish on fact – is revealed by his comment on the story. 'It is experience pushed a little (and only very little) beyond the actual facts of the case for the perfectly legitimate, I believe, purpose of bringing it home to the minds and bosoms of the reader.'

Mystery – it is the Conradian word. But there is no mystery in the work itself, the things imagined; mystery remains a concept of the writer's. The theme of passion and the abyss recurs in Conrad, but there is nothing in his work like the evening scene in Ibsen's *Ghosts*: the lamp being lit, the champagne being called for, light and champagne only underlining the blight of that house, a blight that at first seems external and arbitrary and is then seen to come from within. There is no scene like that, which takes us beyond what we witness and becomes a symbol for aspects of our own experience. There is nothing – still on the theme of blight – like 'The Withered Arm', Hardy's story of rejection and revenge and the dereliction of the innocent, which goes beyond the country tale of magic on which it was based. Conrad is too particular and concrete a writer for that; he sticks too close to the facts; if he had meditated on those stories he might have turned them into case histories.

With writers like Ibsen and Hardy, fantasy answers impulses and needs they might not have been able to state. The truths of that fantasy we have to work out, or translate, for ourselves. With Conrad the process is reversed. We almost begin with the truths – portable truths, as it were, that can sometimes be rendered as aphorisms – and work through to their demonstration. The method was forced on him by the special circumstances that made him a writer. To understand the difficulties of this method, the extraordinary qualities of intelligence and sympathy it required, and the exercise of what he described as the 'poetic faculty', we should try and look at the problem from Conrad's point of view. There is an early story which enables us to do just that.

The story is 'The Return', which was written at the same time as 'Karain'. It is set in London and, interestingly, its two characters are English. Alvan Hervey is a City man. He is 'tall, well set-up, good-looking and healthy; and his clear pale face had under its commonplace refinement that slight tinge of overbearing brutality which is given by the possession of only partly difficult accomplishments; by excelling in games, or in the art of making money; by the easy mastery over animals and over needy men'. And it is already clear that this is less a portrait than an aphorism and an idea about the middle class.

We follow Hervey home one evening. We go up to his dressing room, gaslit, with a butterfly-shaped flame coming out of the mouth of a bronze dragon. The room is full of mirrors and it is suddenly satisfactorily full of middle-class Alvan Herveys. But there is a letter on his wife's dressing table: she has left him. We follow Hervey then through every detail of his middle-class reaction: shock, nausea, humiliation, anger, sadness: paragraph after ordered paragraph, page after page. And, wonderfully, by his sheer analytical intelligence Conrad holds us.

Someone is then heard to enter the house. It is Hervey's wife: she has not, after all, had the courage to leave. What follows now is even more impressive. We move step by step with Hervey, from the feeling of relief and triumph and the wish to punish, to the conviction that the woman, a stranger after five years of marriage, 'had in her hands an indispensable gift which nothing else on earth could give'. So Hervey arrives at the 'irresistible belief in an enigma ... the conviction that within his reach and passing away from him was the very secret of existence – its certitude, immaterial and precious'. He wants then to 'compel the surrender of the gift'. He tells his wife he loves her; but the shoddy words only awaken her indignation, her contempt for the 'materialism' of men, and her anger at her own self-deception. Up to this point the story works. Now it fades away. Hervey remembers that his wife has not had the courage to leave; he feels that she doesn't have the 'gift' which he now needs. And it is he who leaves and doesn't return.

Mysterious words are repeated in this story – 'enigma', 'certitude, immaterial and precious'. But there is no real narrative and no real mystery. Another writer might have charted a course of events. For Conrad, though, the drama and the truth lay not in events but in the analysis: identifying the stages of consciousness through which a passionless man might move to the recognition of the importance of passion. It was the most difficult way of handling the subject; and Conrad suffered during the writing of the eighty-page story. He wrote to Edward Garnett: 'It has embittered five months of my life.' Such a labour; and yet, in spite of the intelligence and real perceptions, in spite of the cinematic details – the mirrors, the bronze dragon breathing fire – 'The Return' remains less a story than an imaginative essay. A truth, as Conrad sees it, has been analysed. But the people remain abstractions.

And that gives another clue. The vision of middle-class people as being all alike, all consciously passionless, delightful and materialist, so that even marriage is like a conspiracy – that is the satirical vision of the outsider.

The year before, when he was suffering with *The Rescue*, Conrad had written to Garnett: 'Other writers have some starting point. Something to catch hold of ... They lean on dialect – or on tradition – or on history – or on the prejudice or fad of the hour; they trade upon some tie or conviction of their time – or upon the absence of these things – which they can abuse or praise. But at any rate they know something to begin with – while I don't. I have had some impressions, some sensations – in my time ... And it's all faded.'

It is the complaint of a writer who is missing a society, and is beginning to understand that fantasy or imagination can move more freely within a closed and ordered world. Conrad's experience was too scattered; he knew many societies by their externals, but he knew none in depth. His human comprehension was complete. But when he set 'The Return' in London he was immediately circumscribed. He couldn't risk much; he couldn't exceed his knowledge. A writer's disadvantage, when the work is done, can appear as advantages. 'The Return' takes us behind the scenes early on, as it were, and gives us some idea of the necessary oddity of the work, and the prodigious labour that lay behind the novels which still stand as a meditation on our world.

It is interesting to reflect on writers' myths. With Conrad there is the imperialist myth of the man of honour, the stylist of the sea. It misses the best of Conrad, but it at least reflects the work. The myths of great writers usually have to do with their work rather than their lives. More and more today, writers' myths are about the writers themselves; the work has become less obtrusive. The great societies that produced the great novels of the past have cracked. Writing has become more private and more privately glamorous. The novel as a form no longer carries conviction. Experimentation, not aimed at the real difficulties, has corrupted response; and there is a great confusion in the minds of readers and writers about the purpose of the novel. The novelist, like the painter, no longer recognizes his interpretive function; he seeks to go beyond it; and his audience diminishes. And so the world we inhabit, which is always new, goes by unexamined, made ordinary by the camera, unmeditated on; and there is no one to awaken the sense of true wonder. That is perhaps a fair definition of the novelist's purpose, in all ages.

Conrad died fifty years ago. In those fifty years his work has penetrated to many corners of the world which he saw as dark. It is a subject for Conradian meditation; it tells us something about our new world. Perhaps it doesn't matter what we say about Conrad; it is enough that he is discussed. You will remember that for Marlow in *Heart of Darkness*, 'the meaning of an episode was not inside like a kernel but outside, enveloping the tale which brought it out only as a glow brings out a haze, in the likeness of one of those misty halos that sometimes are made visible by the spectral illumination of moonshine'.

FOR THE BEST IN PAPERBACKS, LOOK FOR THE 🐧

In every corner of the world, on every subject under the sun, Penguin represents quality and variety – the very best in publishing today.

For complete information about books available from Penguin – including Pelicans, Puffins, Peregrines and Penguin Classics – and how to order them, write to us at the appropriate address below. Please note that for copyright reasons the selection of books varies from country to country.

In the United Kingdom: For a complete list of books available from Penguin in the U.K., please write to *Dept E.P., Penguin Books Ltd, Harmondsworth, Middlesex, UB7 0DA*

In the United States: For a complete list of books available from Penguin in the U.S., please write to *Dept BA, Penguin, 299 Murray Hill Parkway, East Rutherford, New Jersey 07073*

In Canada: For a complete list of books available from Penguin in Canada, please write to *Penguin Books Canada Ltd, 2801 John Street, Markham, Ontario L3R 1B4*

In Australia: For a complete list of books available from Penguin in Australia, please write to the *Marketing Department, Penguin Books Australia Ltd, P.O. Box 257, Ringwood, Victoria 3134*

In New Zealand: For a complete list of books available from Penguin in New Zealand, please write to the *Marketing Department, Penguin Books (NZ) Ltd, Private Bag, Takapuna, Auckland 9*

In India: For a complete list of books available from Penguin, please write to *Penguin Overseas Ltd, 706 Eros Apartments, 56 Nehru Place, New Delhi, 110019*

In Holland: For a complete list of books available from Penguin in Holland, please write to *Penguin Books Nederland B.V., Postbus 195, NL–1380 AD Weesp, Netherlands*

In Germany: For a complete list of books available from Penguin, please write to *Penguin Books Ltd, Friedrichstrasse 10 – 12, D–6000 Frankfurt Main 1, Federal Republic of Germany*

In Spain: For a complete list of books available from Penguin in Spain, please write to *Longman Penguin España, Calle San Nicolas 15, E–28013 Madrid, Spain*

A CHOICE OF PENGUIN FICTION

Monsignor Quixote   Graham Greene

Now filmed for television, Graham Greene's novel, like Cervantes's seventeenth-century classic, is a brilliant fable for its times. 'A deliciously funny novel' – *The Times*

The Dearest and the Best   Leslie Thomas

In the spring of 1940 the spectre of war turned into grim reality – and for all the inhabitants of the historic villages of the New Forest it was the beginning of the most bizarre, funny and tragic episode of their lives. 'Excellent' – *Sunday Times*

Earthly Powers   Anthony Burgess

Anthony Burgess's magnificent masterpiece, an enthralling, epic narrative spanning six decades and spotlighting some of the most vivid events and characters of our times. 'Enormous imagination and vitality . . . a huge book in every way' – Bernard Levin in the *Sunday Times*

The Penitent   Isaac Bashevis Singer

From the Nobel Prize-winning author comes a powerful story of a man who has material wealth but feels spiritually impoverished. 'Singer . . . restates with dignity the spiritual aspirations and the cultural complexities of a lifetime, and it must be said that in doing so he gives the Evil One no quarter and precious little advantage' – Anita Brookner in the *Sunday Times*

Paradise Postponed   John Mortimer

'Hats off to John Mortimer. He's done it again' – *Spectator*. A rumbustious, hilarious new novel from the creator of Rumpole, *Paradise Postponed* was made into a major Thames Television series.

The Balkan Trilogy and Levant Trilogy   Olivia Manning

'The finest fictional record of the war produced by a British writer. Her gallery of personages is huge, her scene painting superb, her pathos controlled, her humour quiet and civilized' – *Sunday Times*

A CHOICE OF PENGUIN FICTION

Maia   Richard Adams

The heroic romance of love and war in an ancient empire from one of our greatest storytellers. 'Enormous and powerful' – *Financial Times*

The Warning Bell   Lynne Reid Banks

A wonderfully involving, truthful novel about the choices a woman must make in her life – and the price she must pay for ignoring the counsel of her own heart. 'Lynne Reid Banks knows how to get to her reader: this novel grips like Super Glue' – *Observer*

Doctor Slaughter   Paul Theroux

Provocative and menacing – a brilliant dissection of lust, ambition and betrayal in 'civilized' London. 'Witty, chilly, exuberant, graphic' – *The Times Literary Supplement*. Now filmed as *Half Moon Street*.

Wise Virgin   A. N. Wilson

Giles Fox's work on the Pottle manuscript, a little-known thirteenth-century tract on virginity, leads him to some innovative research on the subject that takes even his breath away. 'A most elegant and chilling comedy' – *Observer* Books of the Year

Last Resorts   Clare Boylan

Harriet loved Joe Fisher for his ordinariness – for his ordinary suits and hats, his ordinary money and his ordinary mind, even for his ordinary wife. 'An unmitigated delight' – *Time Out*

Trade Wind   M. M. Kaye

An enthralling blend of history, adventure and romance from the author of the bestselling *The Far Pavilions*

A CHOICE OF PENGUIN FICTION

Stanley and the Women   Kingsley Amis

Just when Stanley Duke thinks it safe to sink into middle age, his son goes insane – and Stanley finds himself beset on all sides by women, each of whom seems to have an intimate acquaintance with madness. 'Very good, very powerful . . . beautifully written' – Anthony Burgess in the *Observer*

The Girls of Slender Means   Muriel Spark

A world and a war are winding up with a bang, and in what is left of London all the nice people are poor – and about to discover how different the new world will be. 'Britain's finest post-war novelist' – *The Times*

Him with His Foot in His Mouth   Saul Bellow

A collection of first-class short stories. 'If there is a better living writer of fiction, I'd very much like to know who he or she is' – *The Times*

Mother's Helper   Maureen Freely

A superbly biting and breathtakingly fluent attack on certain libertarian views, blending laughter, delight, rage and amazement, this is a novel you won't forget. 'A winner' – *The Times Literary Supplement*

Decline and Fall   Evelyn Waugh

A comic yet curiously touching account of an innocent plunged into the sham, brittle world of high society. Evelyn Waugh's first novel brought him immediate public acclaim and is still a classic of its kind.

Stars and Bars   William Boyd

Well-dressed, quite handsome, unfailingly polite and charming, who would guess that Henderson Dores, the innocent Englishman abroad in wicked America, has a guilty secret? 'Without doubt his best book so far . . . made me laugh out loud' – *The Times*

A CHOICE OF PENGUIN FICTION

The Ghost Writer Philip Roth

Philip Roth's celebrated novel about a young writer who meets and falls in love with Anne Frank in New England – or so he thinks. 'Brilliant, witty and extremely elegant' – *Guardian*

Small World David Lodge

Shortlisted for the 1984 Booker Prize, *Small World* brings back Philip Swallow and Maurice Zapp for a jet-propelled journey into hilarity. The most brilliant and also the funniest novel that he has written' – *London Review of Books*

Treasures of Time Penelope Lively

Beautifully written, acutely observed, and filled with Penelope Lively's sharp but compassionate wit, *Treasures of Time* explores the relationship between the lives we live and the lives we think we live.

Absolute Beginners Colin MacInnes

The first 'teenage' novel, the classic of youth and disenchantment, *Absolute Beginners* is part of MacInnes's famous London trilogy – and now a brilliant film. 'MacInnes caught it first – and best' – *Harpers and Queen*

July's People Nadine Gordimer

Set in South Africa, this novel gives us an unforgettable look at the terrifying, tacit understanding and misunderstandings between blacks and whites. 'This is the best novel that Miss Gordimer has ever written' – Alan Paton in the *Saturday Review*

The Ice Age Margaret Drabble

'A continuously readable, continuously surprising book . . . here is a novelist who is not only popular and successful but formidably growing towards real stature' – *Observer*

A CHOICE OF PENGUIN FICTION

Money Martin Amis

Savage, audacious and demonically witty – a story of urban excess. 'Terribly, terminally funny: laughter in the dark, if ever I heard it' – *Guardian*

Lolita Vladimir Nabokov

Shot through with Nabokov's mercurial wit, quicksilver prose and intoxicating sensuality, *Lolita* is one of the world's great love stories. 'A great book' – Dorothy Parker

Dinner at the Homesick Restaurant Anne Tyler

Through every family run memories which bind them together – in spite of everything. 'She is a witch. Witty, civilized, curious, with her radar ears and her quill pen dipped on one page in acid and on the next in orange liqueur . . . a wonderful writer' – John Leonard in *The New York Times*

Glitz Elmore Leonard

Underneath the Boardwalk, a lot of insects creep. But the creepiest of all was Teddy. 'After finishing *Glitz*, I went out to the bookstore and bought everything else of Elmore Leonard I could find' – Stephen King

The Battle of Pollocks Crossing J. L. Carr

Shortlisted for the Booker McConnell Prize, this is a moving, comic masterpiece. 'Wayward, ambiguous, eccentric . . . a fascinatingly outlandish novel' – *Guardian*

The Dreams of an Average Man Dyan Sheldon

Tony Rivera is lost. Sandy Grossman Rivera is leaving. And Maggie Kelly is giving up. In the steamy streets of summertime Manhattan, the refugees of the sixties generation wonder what went wrong. 'Satire, dramatic irony and feminist fun . . . lively, forceful and funny' – *Listener*